To Share
in the Body

To Share
in the Body

CRAIG HOVEY

BrazosPress
Grand Rapids, Michigan

© 2008 by Craig Hovey

Published by Brazos Press
a division of Baker Publishing Group
P.O. Box 6287, Grand Rapids, MI 49516-6287
www.brazospress.com

Printed in the United States of America

Library of Congress Cataloging-in-Publication Data
Hovey, Craig, 1974–
    To share in the body / Craig Hovey.
      p.   cm.
    Includes bibliographical references and index.
    ISBN 978-1-58743-217-0 (pbk.)
      1. Martyrdom—Christianity. 2. Martyrdom—Biblical teaching.
    3. Identification (Religion)—Biblical teaching. 4. Bible. N.T. Mark—
Criticism, interpretation, etc. I. Title.
    BR1601.3.H68 2007
    272—dc22   2007020194

To the people of
St. Mark's parish, Newnham, Cambridge, UK

Contents

FOREWORD

SAMUEL WELLS

This is an unusual book. Its style is unusual because there is no attempt to woo the reader. Most books assume the reader is easily bored or generally skeptical. To address the former, the conventional author makes the material skip along with anecdotes and illustrations, showing that this strange material is really not so strange, this daunting document is really quite approachable, this searching writer is really just like you. To address the latter, the author adds countless footnotes, showing that this argument may be far-fetched but look at all the people who agree with it, that this new term may sound pretentious or esoteric but see how resonant it is with the tradition or the contemporary idiom, that this writer is at home in—indeed, at the center of—the debates that matter in the relevant field.

Craig Hovey does not assume his reader is bored or skeptical. His style is probing, piercing, and profound. He makes no apology and asks no permission. He does not make it easy for the reader: there are no little asides that distract from the depth of the study or deflate the seriousness of the message. This is a book about death, and what it might mean to die in faith yet without knowing one's life or death has mattered. One cannot lose sight of the intention of this study for one moment.

It is not just the style of the book that is unusual: it is also the content. For most readers and many theologians, Mark's Gospel is a problem. The problem is what it lacks. For the life coach and the self-help program, it seems to lack easily transferable tips for contemporary application. For the feel-good megachurch, it seems to lack a bright, positive frame of mind. For the historical critic, it seems to lack large chunks of Matthew and Luke, and in particular a proper ending. For Craig Hovey, however, Mark's Gospel lacks nothing. There is no problem with Mark's Gospel: the problem lies with us.

What Mark wants of us is to walk a steep and narrow way. On the one side, temptation lies in making the gospel story simply knowledge or information about God that does not seriously need to cost us anything. To be a martyr is to believe that the gospel must cost us, and if it cost Jesus everything it must cost us everything too. On the other side, an equal temptation lies in making such cost to us what the gospel is about, in coming to assume that the gospel is really about our sacrifice, in making ourselves the center of the story. To be a martyr is to be one who sees, to be one who watches with loving attention, the truth of God in such a way that such truth remains a gift and never becomes a possession. The path between these two temptations is a narrow one, and few have traced its course with more subtlety than this author in this book.

Craig acknowledges that for a contemporary scholar— particularly a white Western male—to speak in depth of martyrdom is to risk misunderstanding or even ridicule.

But he sees this as no reason to be silent. He writes not to exalt or privilege his own context but to expose the demands and the glory of the gospel. Mark's Gospel is not fundamentally about the circumstances in which Jesus finds us: it is about the trajectory on which Jesus sends us. It is this trajectory, shown in all its color through the prism of blundering disciples, perceptive blind people, impetuous intimates, and flawed followers, that Craig explores in unrelenting logic. *To Share in the Body* is above all a work of logic—theo-logic—that takes the promise of Jesus at face value and arranges all other goods in its train.

I recall that after the disclosure of the torture taking place at Abu Ghraib prison in Iraq in 2004, I felt the best way to preach was not simply to denounce the horrific practices and the culture that made them imaginable. Such was timely and appropriate but did not seem to be the stuff of a sermon. Instead I wondered aloud whether if our country were invaded by a foreign power, we—the congregation and I—would be considered enough of a threat to be worth torturing. Not a political threat, necessarily, and probably not a military threat, but a living presence of hope and truth whose continued witness would become intolerable to an invader bent on submission and destruction. This, I sense, is the tenor of Craig Hovey's argument throughout *To Share in the Body*: to make God's people a disciplined and responsive community whose witness constitutes a rival claim to truth that unsettles the forces that this book describes as "instrumentalism" and the "world."

Craig was a member of the congregation that heard the Abu Ghraib sermon. Many times I have had the privilege of worshiping and studying and discerning with him. One thing I most cherish about Craig is the way he leads public prayers. His prayers are like this

11

book—searching, uncompromising, unsettling, and wise. This kind of writing, it seems to me, is a matter of digging into the heart of God, and as such is a form of prayer. For many of us, prayer is a list of woes, a few mercies, and an effort to concentrate. But this book points to a richer form of prayer—profound attention to the character of God met in Christ, and a sustained effort to follow the logic of God's call in its personal, political, and cosmic dimensions.

And that may mean that some who read this book may come to be martyrs. So one should read this book with fear and trembling, as well as joy.

PREFACE

L iving among Anglicans for a time, I came to appreciate the words that make the title of this book. "We
break this bread to share in the body of Christ." I
came to see these words from the liturgy of Common
Worship as the center of the universe. In the middle of
the eucharistic celebration, the festival of praise, the
people of God rejoice that the body of Christ was torn;
we also tear it anew, and share in it. There is no activity
more central to the life of the church, the proclamation
of the kingdom come in Christ, or the history of the world
than this one. Still, I suspect that humanity is narcis-
sistic enough gleefully to promote its own words to such
a status. After all, "center of the universe" was only too
readily accepted by earlier generations whose geocentric
dreams underwrote humanity's self-importance.

But they are not our own words. We speak them but
do not know what they mean; they are formed on human
lips, but like a bird from a cage, they immediately take
flight and escape our grasp. It is quite a discipline to
keep speaking words that will not be reined in. Yet this
is the mystery and the gift of Christ to the world and

13

to a church that would learn to dispossess its own witness and wait on the promise of God. This book is an attempt to think through how the witness of martyrs is just such a witness, and how this is not only the business of a select few but the shape of the body in which all Christians share.

Any book on martyrdom will understandably invite scrutiny as to the context of its composition. That I wrote this book on the placid banks of the River Cam, at great remove from personal threat of persecution, accurately reflects my inability to speak with firsthand experience about martyrdom. I am disqualified, though not uniquely so, from telling the stories of martyrs personally known to me, since I do not personally know any martyrs. Nevertheless, this admission appropriately locates the central concern of this book: to reimagine what it means for *every* church to be a martyr-church.

I accept that there is a kind of contradiction between the context of this book's composition and the state of affairs it conceives of as normative for the church: its suffering in a hostile world for the sake of its gospel proclamation. But I do not accept that it falls only to others to reflect on the meaning of martyrdom as a New Testament assumption and mandate. Instead, I have tried to take seriously a responsibility I believe to be incumbent on all Christians including those in first-world comfort: to refuse to relegate the threat of martyrdom to the fringes of history or remote parts of the globe. The church may well discover that some settings are more hostile than others, that the world exhibits more and less hospitality to Christ's heralds depending on the mode of its witness, the whims of rulers, and a multitude of other factors. But it is my conviction that the periods and places of quiet are exceptions to the rule and more often reflect the church's willingness to accommodate to its host culture than indicate that culture's inherent goodness.

There is another irony that has accompanied the writing of this book. I wrote during Lent, a time of the church's preparation, its self-denial for the sake of following Jesus to the cross, its resolve not to abandon Jesus to die alone. Yet as this also coincided with the final weeks of awaiting the arrival of my first child, I have discovered in Lent this year a curious kind of preparation. It is a present haunted by the shadow of an impending future marked by death and betrayal. The purple and then red trappings of the altar seem almost to darken further still at the start of Holy Week. And yet this year for me the Lenten present has also been strangely pregnant with a different sort of future, one of new life and promise, lightness and joyful anticipation. Perhaps this is what it means for the church to look toward Good Friday and Easter beyond it with a combination of terror and ecstasy. Maybe it captures the wonderful contradiction of living ready for death yet having so much to live for, the irresolvable divergence of cross and resurrection. And—though I hesitate even to speak it as if I may spoil a great secret—possibly it invites us to share in the hope of martyrs.

Craig Hovey
Holy Week, 2006

15

Introduction

It is widely believed that Mark's Gospel was written for a persecuted church at a violent time in history. Its aim is to help Christians who are struggling against oppression and forces that attempt to silence the preaching of the gospel. In short, it was written for a martyr-church.

This immediately raises a question about the extent to which such a Gospel can be "for us." On the one hand, Christians confess that the Bible is different from every other piece of literature because it alone is the church's scripture. It is circularly called scripture and read accordingly by a people who have been formed by reading it together. Whether and how its message is for Christians who find themselves living the Christian faith in a variety of times and places will depend on how the churches allow their common life to be shaped by faithful practices. If persecution is not a characteristic of our cultural-historical moment, the church may nevertheless embody the witness of martyrs when it does not allow that moment to define the sweep of its obedience or the extent of its discipleship. This reflects the conviction that martyrdom is neither contrived nor an exact opposition to unbelief, but is instead a gift of God to the church. Such a gift funds the church's ability to recall its fallen members as part of its ongoing existence and witness.[1]

In this book, I attempt to take seriously the fact that, like all of the Bible, the Gospel of Mark belongs to the church. If it was indeed originally written to a martyr-church, I have tried to resist the temptation to think that this means that it was written for someone else. I have refused to accept with any ease that the import of this Gospel, when it assumes persecution, is irrelevant to some Christians and is only for those on the fringes. Mark's theology of martyrdom does not cease to be true when nonmartyrs read it. Neither should Mark's Gospel be read as a fanatical or obsessive time capsule by those who cannot immediately identify themselves as heroes in its narrative. For one thing, no living Christian can know that she will not be remembered by the church as a martyr, because, short of suicide (see chapter 2), no living Christian can know her fate ahead of time. This means that, so long as we assume that "we" are not a martyr-church, we have ceased to live with a proper and appropriate antagonism to the world in attempts to preclude the possibility that we might die the death of Christ. We have secured our own fates as nonmartyrs.

Against this tendency, I invite readers to view the Christian life as an adventure of faith that is rooted in the church's witness to the world. As such, martyrdom is not witness gone terribly wrong but its ultimate paradigm. Martyrs have not failed in their proclamation; their deaths are found within the very substance of the

1. Dietrich Bonhoeffer speaks about martyrdom as a gift in this way. See *The Cost of Discipleship*, trans. R. H. Fuller (New York: Touchstone, 1995), 89.

gospel proclaimed. This is the gospel proclaimed by all Christians who include in their proclamation the work of remembering those who have died in their witness. To take part in this work and this witness is therefore to acknowledge that "martyr-church" identifies the locus of Christian life for all who follow Christ.

Let us be very clear. Not every Christian will be killed for their faith. But since no single Christian can know whether they will be killed for their faith until the actual moment of death, martyrdom is a real possibility for every living Christian. This admittedly sounds slightly absurd, though it may make some logical sense. Surely we can know with greater probability than this that most Western Christians especially will not undergo martyrdom. This is almost certainly right, and yet we must subsequently be careful not to view martyrdom as a feature of the world, even when it is only rarely found in it. Instead, martyrdom is an aspect of the gospel in the world, an intrinsic quality of the cross of Christ, and therefore a mark of the church both in how it remembers those who have died and in how it prepares and trains its members for faithfulness. This book attempts to think through this perplexing truth by taking for granted that every church is meant to be a martyr-church despite the fact that not every Christian's witness will be a martyr-witness.

In what follows, I make deliberate and self-conscious use of the Bible, primarily through a careful reading of martyrdom in Mark's Gospel. There is an unfortunate division between the Bible and theology that is possibly better known in the academy than in many churches. Following more than a century of historical criticism, the bulk of biblical scholarship is still shaped by the assumption that the meaning of the Bible is to be found with scientific instruments. The limits of science and the secularity of this assumption make plain that this is both unlikely and unfaithful. But rather than reproduce many of the arguments of the last fifty years that have exposed the inherent inadequacies of historical criticism, I have chosen instead to proceed with a theological mode of reading the Gospel that assumes the truth of the Gospel. I have not questioned its recorded events on historical grounds. Nor have I looked for any meaning behind the text, since any such meaning will always involve an appeal to something other than the church's scripture.

Moreover, as a Christian theologian, I have tried to write in an attempt to read the Bible theologically. I have not assumed that theology and biblical studies identify two independent discourses. Mark did not have Nicaea, Athanasius, or the Cappadocians, but he is nevertheless part of the same church, and certainly his book is as much their book. It is also as much our book as it was Mark's. For instance, if Mark is part of the scripture of those who worship God as Father, Son, and Holy Spirit, then Christians ought to expect to find the Trinity in Mark.

This naturally has its limits. For one thing, there is a literary unity to Mark that should be respected. There are wonderful patterns of symbols and evocative images that reappear throughout the narrative as markers for close readers. Part of reading with care is paying particular attention to the subtleties. Doing so also means respecting the message of Mark's story on its own before too quickly filling in the gaps with material from the other Gospels. In this respect, while we interpret in light of the church's worship and the use of the Bible in the life of faith, we must also take care not to overpower fragile intertextual connections and the delicately crafted turns in the plot. So even though we should expect to find the Trinity in Mark, we must not privilege our perception of it in advance of

20

our reading. We ought to allow Mark's Gospel to disclose even yet more insights—even, and especially, regarding those things that we have inherited as the church's tradition, not because we do not trust our forebears but precisely because Mark himself was one of them.

I have made the following assumptions in my reading:

1. Mark was written for the whole church of Jesus Christ. This means that it was written neither for me as an individual Christian nor for a particular church in the first century. To be sure, a first-century church may have been the first to read it, but because it exists as the church's scripture for all time, it at the very least is a reminder that no historical epoch can lay claim to its definitive meaning without implying that it is for them and not for others.

2. Martyrdom is a possibility for all Christians because the church of Jesus Christ is a martyr-church. This means that Mark's allusions to martyrdom are not historical relics but the shape of the Good News for those who would take up their cross and follow Jesus. Even though Mark may well have written his Gospel during a dangerous period, the church does not have the luxury of confining its meaning to that period.

3. It is neither possible nor desirable to know what "Mark thought." What the church has is its scripture, not the mind of an author. Historical criticism has been terribly wrong to think that an author's motivation or intention provides clues for understanding what is written. When the New Testament makes surprising use of Old Testament texts by seeing Jesus Christ in them, has it departed from the true meaning of the texts or discovered it? Has it violated a cardinal rule of biblical interpretation or called that rule into question? Such queries can be answered only by and for the people who are willing to own the reading of their scriptures in their worship.

21

4. Christian scripture exists first for the formation of the life of Christian worship. For example, the Psalms are first to be sung and to be studied in the midst of that singing and for the sake of those who sing them. Likewise, the Gospels are liturgical texts, elevated in worship, read aloud in common, and discerned for their meaning in living the Christian life through the church. The church cannot control how God speaks through the scriptures, because its first encounter with them is the definitive one: the receptivity and vulnerability of lives laid open in adoration.

5. The Bible does not exist in order to answer our questions. It does not grant legitimacy to those things that we deem worth asking about, those things that we take to be of fundamental importance. Instead, the Bible questions our questions by querying us and then often waiting in silence while we clamor and struggle to prepare an adequate answer. For example, Mark will not answer the obvious question "Who is Jesus?" in an obvious way nor in a way that allows those who ask it to evade the question of their own identity. This is not to say that questions about Jesus are really questions about us; it only indicates that we do not ask about Jesus with impunity.

In what follows, my goal is to identify and elaborate some of the themes and images relevant to the display of martyrdom in the Gospel. The material is structured around six key moments: baptism (chapter 1), the call to take up crosses and follow Jesus (chapter 2), the transfiguration (chapter 3), deserting Jesus in the garden (chapter 4), the crucifixion (chapter 5), and the empty tomb (chapter 6). The final chapter then takes stock of what it means to be a martyr-church today.

Sharing in the body of Christ is the work and joy of all Christians. That it is difficult is known because it involves carrying crosses. That it is joyful is known because it involves believing promises.

I

THE WATERS
THAT DROWN

To share in the body is to enact and declare membership with a martyr-church. It is to relate one's identity to a determination that exists beyond oneself without excluding oneself. It is to entrust one's future to God and to others who likewise entrust their future to God. It is to subject one's loves and fears to an overriding mission in which both love and fear are transformed and redeemed. To share in the body is to reassess the primacy of the individual body in view of the new body God is creating through the salvation of the world in Christ. It is to proceed on the basis of trust in promises. It is not to assess risk and safety on the basis of reason but to hope for presence on the basis of faithfulness.

Sharing in the body of Christ occurs first in baptism. In Mark's Gospel, Jesus describes his own death and those of two confused disciples in these terms. The meaning of baptism for Christians, therefore, must pass through this reference.

> And taking the twelve again, he began to tell them what was to happen to him, saying, "Behold, we are going up to Jerusalem; and the Son of man will be delivered to the chief priests and the scribes, and they will condemn him to death, and deliver him to the Gentiles; and they will mock him, and spit upon him, and scourge him, and kill him; and after three days he will rise." And James and John, the sons of Zebedee, came forward to him, and said to him, "Teacher, we want you to do for us whatever we ask of you." And he said to them, "What do you want me to do for you?" And they said to him, "Grant us to sit, one at your right hand and one at your left, in your glory." But Jesus said to them, "You do not know what you are asking. Are you able to drink the cup that I drink, or to be baptized with the baptism with which I am baptized?" And they said to him, "We are able." And Jesus said to them, "The cup that I drink you will drink; and with the baptism with which I am baptized, you will be baptized; but to sit at my right hand or at my left is not mine to grant, but it is for those for whom it has been prepared." (10:32–40)

Though it was not obvious to James and John, it is clear to the reader: baptism is equated with the suffering and death of the cross, just as the cross is equated with glory. Thus there is an accompanying warning that to misunderstand that the cross is the height of glory will also be to misunderstand what is involved in baptism. If there can be no glory without the cross, there can be no baptism without the suffering that discipleship names as a function of bearing one's cross.[1]

Observing these things immediately throws us into the symbolic and intense world of Mark's Gospel: the way of the cross is suffering; it is not just for Jesus but for all disciples; the cross itself is glory though it looks like anything but this; to be baptized is to die. In particular, the rite of Christian initiation displays several characteristics that will help to show how it is bound up with martyrdom.[2]

Christian baptism makes a double reference: it is both a cleansing and a drowning. Washing the body is a kind of purification for what comes next. The baptisms performed by John the Baptist in the Judean wilderness deepened the traditional ritual cleansing to include the purity of the heart as well. The whole person, not just the skin, was subject to this cleansing. In Mark, John baptizes with a "baptism of repentance for the forgiveness of sins" (1:4). But this was only in preparation for what was to come, to prepare the way of the Lord and to attune the crowds to the One who would come after John. "After me comes he who is mightier than I, the thong of whose sandals I am not worthy to stoop down and untie. I have baptized you with water; but he will baptize you with the Holy Spirit" (1:7–8). A baptism that is only with water is a baptism of cleansing.

1. John Howard Yoder discusses the difficulty the Emmaus disciples had in seeing the cross as the height of glory in *The Politics of Jesus*, 2nd ed. (Grand Rapids: Eerdmans, 2000), 51.

2. Herbert McCabe discusses the paradoxes of suffering and glory, further observing that by the time Mark wrote these words, James had already been martyred in Jerusalem. See *God, Christ, and Us* (New York: Continuum, 2003), 43. This is, of course, a double paradox, since Jesus's reply exposes James's and John's misunderstanding, only to affirm for us that they had spoken the truth despite themselves.

But Christian baptism is also a kind of drowning. In being baptized by John, Jesus underwent the baptism of purification, but this action coincided with the action of God in sending the Holy Spirit to alight on Jesus like a dove (1:10). Even though Jesus does not literally baptize anyone in Mark's Gospel, the reference John makes to the baptism Jesus will enact "with the Holy Spirit," together with the presence of the Spirit at Jesus's own baptism, makes an unmistakable connection between those who will follow Jesus and the way that they will somehow share in his baptism. We have seen how, in Mark 10, Jesus will later relate his baptism to his death and include his disciples in its logic. This is what is meant by being identified with Christ in his death and resurrection. It also explains another difference between John's baptism and Christian baptism. The latter is the rite of initiation into a new people made by the Holy Spirit on account of their sharing in the death and resurrection of Christ. To be baptized with Christ is to be baptized into his death, as Paul writes (Rom. 6:3). The surging waters of the baptismal do not only cleanse, they kill; they do not only wash the body, they destroy it. The white gown of the new initiate is the color of martyrs.[3] As we will see later, this is the color worn by Christ at the transfiguration and by the young man symbolizing the church at the empty tomb, both having been killed and raised, both having been martyred.

3. For this reason, Thomas Aquinas held that one who shares in Christ's suffering may receive the sacramental effect of a water baptism without undergoing physical baptism (*Summa Theologiae* 3.66.11). Commenting on this tradition, Karl Rahner observes that "in martyrdom, what had previously been signified and made present through the sacramental sign of baptism is here simply fulfilled" (*On the Theology of Death* [New York: Herder and Herder, 1961], 102–3). He goes on to say that even though martyrdom cannot be called a sacrament in the normal sense, this is not because it is less than a sacrament, but more.

26

In addition to identifying with the suffering of Christ in being lowered into the deadly waters and also being raised with him, Christian baptism identifies one with the body of Christ, the church. The new body is composed of those who have shed old bodies in the drowning waters and are clothed with new life in a new body—one simultaneously collective and ecclesial. The assembly that gathers at Easter every year differs from the previous year. It is constituted by a new membership as a shifting body, reminded that this community is not based on friendship with one another nor common interests as though it were an elite club. The rich and poor, the important and unimportant of the world, are included in the new community that God has made in the person of Jesus.

In this way, Christian baptism involves identification with two things: with Christ and with the church. But it is important to see how these two aspects are related, how the body of Christ is both suffered with and constituted in baptism. They are distinguishable but not separable. To identify with Christ in his death and resurrection *is* to identify with the church. But this also makes sense only if the church is a martyr-church. What does this mean? It means that the church is characterized by the life of the resurrection only insofar as it undergoes the pain of the cross. The body of Christ crucified and raised is the body of Christ that God has called church.[4]

Even though they do not know what they are asking for, James's and John's baptisms nevertheless make

4. From the opposite side of the logic, Brad S. Gregory cites how Cyprian argued that one needed to be in the church in order to be a martyr. This means that a heretic could still be a martyr, though was devoid of charity on account of rejecting the mystical body of Christ. See Gregory, *Salvation at Stake: Christian Martyrdom in Early Modern Europe* (Cambridge, Mass.: Harvard University Press, 1999), 330.

them members of the community of the cross. To die with Christ is not just to "die to sin." It is also to be realigned with a new people created by God for life in the kingdom in which Christ reigns supreme. Further, it is to be dead to the world, severed from the old allegiances, worldly loyalties, and limited imaginations. It is to be free for the new life named by inclusion in the community of the resurrection, the life of the church, for whom death no longer defines the limit of what is possible. A risen Christ does not simply return to the life he lived before, and in the same way, by sharing in Christ's rising, the church does not merely anticipate "more of the same" for eternity. Instead, it looks forward to a share in a new way of living, a new form of social relations, a new way of dealing with conflict, with power, with domination.

Even though Jesus underwent John's baptism, sharing in the body does not just mean imitating Jesus by being baptized ourselves. Today, the Jordan River is a site of sentimentality for those hoping to make their own baptism there more authentic in this respect. But the authenticity of Christian baptism is not accomplished through reproducing Jesus's baptism by John, for this would be to undergo only the baptism of repentance. Christian baptism is much more than this. One difference is indicated by the descent of the Holy Spirit of whom John spoke: "I have baptized you with water; but he will baptize you with the Holy Spirit" (1:8). The Holy Spirit creates the church, as at Pentecost. It is through baptism by the Holy Spirit that God creates and builds the church, adding members to its ranks. This is the first thing to say about Christian baptism. It marks the inclusion of the individual within the life of the community of faith. The placement of the font in many church buildings is meant to signal this fact. The body is washed upon entering

28

through the doors, though not primarily for cleansing. Indeed, this is how God grows the church.

As we consider how this growth takes place, it is worth noting that one cannot baptize oneself. Entering the church involves subjection to the way of life the church has preserved for disciples. It cannot be made on the basis of a separate assertion or the invention of a better way. To do so would only leave individuals to be their own churches, deprived of the gifts of God made present in the gifts that are the other members of Christ's body. So baptism is a reminder that we cannot partake of the gifts God gives the church apart from being a part of it. The gifts to individual Christians are not sufficient on their own to allow them to live the Christian life. No single Christian is called to do what Jesus did; this is the mission and task of the whole church, the collected gifts of its members, the complete body of Christ.

The most obvious outcome of baptism is the growth of the church. But we might ask whether such growth is a human or a divine work. On the one hand, I have just affirmed not only the presence of the community to the new member but also the work of that community for the new member's inclusion. If there were no church, no present and historic community of believers, there would be no way to extend the church into the future, no connection to the subsequent generation of Christians, no way to establish continuity with those who will come next. With every generation, the church is in danger of extinction. There may be no church after the deaths of living Christians: those things that demonstrate what it means to be a Christian are always one generation from loss unless they are renewed by those who come next. Christian living, worship, the regard for scripture, the demonstration of reading it—these are all practiced in partial view of the fact that those who will learn them

29

today will teach them to others tomorrow. If there are no more learners, tomorrow will be absent the church of God. Responsibility for ensuring the endurance of the church, in this way, appears quite ordinarily human. And in the Gospels, from John's baptism in the Jordan to the command of Christians to make disciples through baptism and teaching Jesus's commands, the rite of Christian initiation appears likewise to be a human work.

But on the other hand, since the church is a creation of the Holy Spirit, the human acts of washing, of wetting, of lowering and raising are made more than merely human acts. The actions of John the Baptist and the descent of the Holy Spirit on Jesus establish the joint work of human and divine agency. This is what it means to call Christian baptism a sacrament. God acts in our acts. Human movements and significances are transformed and lifted up into the divine life, renewed, repaired, and put to use in the service of God. Ordinary movements through the water are met with God's presence through promise. Flawed human creations are made perfect by God's grace, even and especially the recurring, constant creation of the church itself.

The agrarian idiom in Jesus's parables accurately captures the way that the church is a creation of God. While we cannot equate the church with the kingdom, they are both extended by a power that is not given to human exercise.

> The kingdom of God is as if a man should scatter seed upon the ground, and should sleep and rise night and day, and the seed should sprout and grow, he knows not how. The earth produces of itself, first the blade, then the ear, then the full grain in the ear. But when the grain is ripe, at once he puts in the sickle, because the harvest has come. (4:26–29)

30

The inclusion of members in the church is the work of harvesting what has been prepared by unseen forces, the work of God while the church itself sleeps and rises. In this way, the promise of God is like the promise of the earth in perennial produce without the aid of human work.[5]

Still, when the harvest comes, it is itself a mutual, divine-human activity. God adds to the church in the ritual of adding to which we contribute. Participating with the work of God in baptism, the church attests to the way that God's promises invite the work of his people. Such promises are not enacted apart from human agency, God doing God's own work in front of a passive world. Nor are such promises activated only when a corporate human will becomes decisive enough to act in the space and time inhabited by its neighbors. The former refuses to acknowledge that the church is an agent, while the latter mistakes the nature of that agency. The former is a passive church, while the latter is a church devoted to strategy. Each mistakenly assesses its own work. Instead, God's promise to be present to sacramental actions like baptism welcomes human effort to join in the divine drama. The tentative, fragile, and misunderstanding involvement of the church relative to its own continued existence is met with the power that created the universe and continually upholds it.

Even though the church is not guaranteed that it will always extend from one generation to the next, it is promised the Holy Spirit. And insofar as the church is constituted by the presence of that Spirit, the future church is as sure as God's promise. The church is constantly both

5. Here I am following Ched Myers's interpretation of this section when he asserts that "the growth of the kingdom will be neither obvious nor controllable" (*Binding the Strong Man* [Maryknoll, N.Y.: Orbis, 1988], 179).

31

threatened with extinction and promised preservation. It perpetually hangs in the balance but submits to the constant renewal of its community, of its life together, and of its presence gathered in worship. But the connection between the threat and preservation is never resolved by an overwhelming power. God does not meet the risk of extinction by extinguishing the risk. Instead, God promises to enact countervailing acts of creation out of nothing. God's intervention is not characterized by eliminating the church's enemies, prevailing over the factors that imperil its peace. Its peace does not depend on the defeat of its enemies in any normal sense. This is what is celebrated in baptism. It is the fulfillment of God's promise in which the church celebrates both the constant newness of its ranks and the deliberate way that God is saving the world.

Even so, this act of creation, the creation of the church, is never more than the humble addition of one member at a time. The church is not created with the single sweep of an arm, met with an en masse conversion. *World* and *church* are not only collective nouns but collections of human individuals. In baptism, a human individual is transferred from the world to the church. The world registers a loss in loyalty; the church registers an advance in loyalty. The transfer from world to church is slow but celebrative; the preparation may be protracted, but it is resolute.

Because of this shift, baptism marks a definite realignment of power. It is here that we explicitly encounter the connection between martyrdom and baptism. Perhaps the most extreme way that the church encounters extinction is at the hands of a hostile world through persecution and death. If baptism is the way that God creates the church in the Holy Spirit, the deaths of martyrs are its dark parallel and its potential undoing. If the church grows through the initiation of one member at a time, it seemingly shrinks through an equivalent but opposite process. The world attempts to regain its lost members, to secure its former loyalties, and to establish its earlier power. In this way, baptism is an overtly political act. Like the burning of draft cards, baptism declares a switched identity, a refusal to be one thing and a determination to be something else. It should not be surprising, therefore, that Jesus is tempted in the wilderness immediately following his baptism (1:12–13). He engages in a direct confrontation of cosmic, though intensely political, significance. It should not be surprising that the promise of God in the Holy Spirit descended on Jesus would be met by resistance, an attempt to negotiate a treaty, as some of the Gospels tell it (e.g., Luke 4:5–6). Transferring citizenship from one kingdom to another is the action performed in baptism, but it also signals entrance into a temptation to trade the new citizenship back for the old, to render back to the worldly powers the souls of God's people, the church. The most desperate way the world has for attempting this is the martyrdom of Christians.

But just as baptism is not an exclusively human act, so also is martyrdom prevented from effects of mere human hands and wills. The church neither increases nor decreases through human work. In other words, the promise of God to meet the church in the newly baptized member remains with the church even, and especially, in the deaths of its martyrs, that is, in the seeming undoing of the church's enlargement. It is not possible to account for the growth of the church in terms of strategy, ingenuity, or resources. But neither is it possible to account for its destruction at the hands of its enemies in these terms.

This fact points to the way that God is saving the world. Martyrs are promised that their deaths will be instrumental in the repentance of the nations, a promise that can be understood in light of what we have been observing about baptism.[6] It has two aspects. First, contrary to the will of the hostile world, a martyr's death does not reduce the membership of the church, since the dead saints are still members. This is the content of the promise made not only to martyrs but indeed to all Christians at baptism. The body into which the new member is included is a historic body that extends through the ages, comprising those who are living and those who live in the memory and witness of the church as it is instantiated throughout time. Christians are not associated with one another within the church in the same way as, for example, in a marriage, since "till death do us part" makes no reference to the conditions for churchly fellowship. At the least, this is a reminder that our lives are joined to the lives of those who are mostly unknown to us, unchosen by us, and only given to us as brothers and sisters through a common adoption.

Second, when the world persecutes the church, the hostile aims of the world are prevented from having the last word. The promise of God to martyrs turns out actually to be also a promise to the whole world, especially in its hostility. God does not abandon the enemies of Christians to a world bereft of Christian witness. The continuing presence of the church in the world, despite the death of its members and the antagonism of the world, is an aspect of God's baptismal promise. Despite its efforts, the world will not be left without the witness of the church, the proclamation of the gospel, the celebration of God's kingdom, and good news to

6. This promise is explicitly made in Revelation 11:1–13.

34

the poor. That this is the case, however, has nothing to do with determination on the part of Christians to overtake the world in power or to subdue it in strength. On the contrary, it has everything to do with the ability of Christians to believe God's promises in baptism: just as God has promised to grow the church through the gift of the Holy Spirit rather than through human efforts, so also has God promised that human efforts to destroy the church will be met with the gratuity of the Spirit's activity.[7]

Of course, such a connection between the growth of the church and the repentance of the nations seems somewhat paradoxical. I have noted that the growth of the church is baptismal and sacramental and that the world's persecutions also must be seen as being included within God's baptismal and sacramental promises. I have also noted that the presence of the church in the world is preserved by God for the sake of the world. This does not mean that there will not be martyrs, only that martyrdom will not silence the witness of God's people but will play a role in the repentance of the nations. But this may appear paradoxical since, in fact, the growth of the church *is* the repentance of the nations; baptism is the way the world repents. Beginning to worship God and to follow Jesus is marked by the initiation of members of the world into the membership of the church. God promises baptism as the result of martyrdom. This seems to imply that when the world kills a martyr, it is furthering *its own* baptism into the body of Christ.

7. It is for this reason that, as J. Warren Smith observes, "the true martyr cannot be motivated by *ressentiment*." Trusting the promises of God to martyrs (and, by extension, to the whole church), martyrs are permitted a spirit of gentleness toward their persecutors. Smith, "Martyrdom: Self-Denial or Self-Exaltation? Motives for Self-Sacrifice from Homer to Polycarp—A Theological Reflection," *Modern Theology* 22, no. 2 (April 2006): 190.

It may be that this relationship between martyrdom and baptism is marked less by paradox than by irony, since it so clearly shares the ironic logic of resurrection. The way the world kills is not finally allowed to be antithetical to the way that God saves. Jesus's words from the cross in Luke, "Father, forgive them; for they know not what they do," can be read as precisely displaying this irony (Luke 23:34). They do not know what they are doing because their killing is becoming the very grounds for the possibility of their forgiveness. When the Father grants the Son's request for forgiveness of his enemies, the Father's answer will be the cross and the resurrection. The ironic logic of this means that the connection between Jesus's death and the forgiveness of the Roman army is the gift of the Father to the Son, which will be good news for the whole world and constitute the content of all Christian proclamation. Martyrs are included in the death and resurrection of Christ because their deaths witness to the Father's gift to the Son by contributing to the growth of the church in baptism. In this way, resurrection explains the connection between martyrdom and baptism.

However, we must register an objection to this way of rendering the connection. It may be the case that God is saving the world through the witness of his martyrs and the mission of the martyr-church. It may also be the case that the nations, despite themselves, are submitting to the divine will in the persecution of God's people, unwittingly strengthening the vehicle for forgiveness it will in time receive, fortifying the mode by which God is building the church in their own attempts to undermine it. But we will rightly object that the overt persecution of the church by the world seems relatively rare. Intolerant tyrants who kill Christians have always been the exception rather than the rule. Most Christians have not had to die for their faith; their deaths have not been a witness to the nations in this sense. What then shall we say about God's promises?

The first thing to say is that martyrdom is not the only mode of witness the church has. Christians bear a positive message to the world. That message speaks of salvation and good news before it speaks about condemnation. The church is not first against the world but for the world. When it encounters hostility in a world that refuses to hear the gospel, the church must have a clear conscience before God that it has not courted that hostility. The New Testament warnings against feeling self-righteous for suffering for doing wrong warn the church of all ages to account its witness a primary value and its suffering a noninstrumental value. Imagining the connection between the Christian experience of suffering and divine approval to be a causal one is only a variation of the mistaken idea that Christian suffering causes the nations to repent. Both are false, but not because there is *no* connection between suffering and approval or suffering and repentance. Instead they are false because such a connection cannot be explained as an internal quality of suffering. The deaths of martyrs are not somehow an evangelistic strategy. With this awareness Christians are released from the thought that persecution is necessary for the church's witness. They are promised that persecution may be an empirical reality but that the salvation of the world does not rely on and depend on the opposition of the world to the kingdom of God.[8]

8. Even though Stephen was the first martyr, he was not the first witness (*marturia*), since not all witnesses are martyrs in this sense. As Barth observes, Stephen is not a martyr because he dies but he dies because he is a witness (*Church Dogmatics* 4/3.2, trans. G. W. Bromiley et al. [Edinburgh: T & T Clark, 1956–75], 611). Here Barth is partly echoing Augustine, who in his exposition of Psalm 34 said that it is the cause for which the martyr dies that makes the

An aspect of this is the affirmation that the power of nations, when it is put to use in killing Christians, is enlisted by God against the will of the nations. What it does not mean is that the power of the nations is necessary for their salvation. The gospel of God curbs the pretense of the powerful by demonstrating that that power is absolutely incidental to the power of God. The power of nations, of its weapons, exists for no reason and serves no purpose. There is no activity that God must accomplish in the world which requires the cooperation of the nations' ability to impose order, to exercise authority, to assemble and mobilize armies, to destroy other nations, to flex their brawn. None of these qualities is an ingredient in the plan of God for the cosmos; none is integral to the way that God has created nor to the way that he continues to uphold creation; none is relevant to establishing justice, rendering mercy, demonstrating love, defending the weak, healing the sick, promoting equality, or bringing peace. The power of nations is just there; it does not exist out of necessity.[9]

---

martyr, not the punishment they suffer. This point served Augustine's and Luther's cases against the Donatists and Anabaptists respectively.

9. I am referring here to what we commonly call "the state" rather than to what the New Testament speaks of as "the nations" (*ethnos*). Nevertheless, in Christ, the relativization of the nations in the latter sense (through the inclusion of Gentiles) surely extends to the very logic of their *existence* as well. Just as the *polis* ceases to be the site of genuine political deliberation once the Spirit of God establishes the church, so also the nations of clan and race no longer hold ontological purchase in view of the new humanity God has created. On the relativization of the *polis*, particularly in Acts, see my "Free Christian Speech: Plundering Foucault," *Political Theology* 8, no. 1 (January 2007): 63–81. If it is no longer possible to account for the existence of states according to what we might call "salvation-necessity," we must surely also cease describing the coercion thought natural to states in necessary terms. This is the meaning of Barth's insistence that violence is an *opus alienun* for the state (*Church Dogmatics* 3/4, 456). Ironically, some attempts to reject the ultimate authority of states on the basis of their coercion dangerously underwrite the existence of states by saying that states are necessarily coercive. Scholars like John Howard Yoder, Jacques Ellul, Vernard Eller, and others who

That God nevertheless enlists the power of nations against the wills of nations is another matter entirely. God does not need the might of the world in order to act in the world. Still, God chooses to make good use of evil, just as the actions of Pharaoh were made to function in the creation of a holy nation for God. God did not need Pharaoh, just as God did not need Rome. Likewise, God did not even need the cross but enlisted it for divine and good purposes. This is the meaning of Paul's much misunderstood claim that governments wield the sword as God's servants (Rom. 13:4). They serve God *against their will*. This is so because the whole universe belongs to God, even the parts of it that are in rebellion, claiming autonomy from God and sole authority over their dominions. Paul's assertion must not be construed as congratulating the nations' goodness and commending their power simply and straightforwardly as a necessary condition of God's way in the world. God's way requires no swords, no crosses, no guns, though these are enslaved and enlisted for divine purposes as an expression of God's sovereignty over human rebellion and pride.

The second thing to say in response to the objection that martyrdom seems rare is to ask whether the world ignores and tolerates the church for the right reasons. Does the world ignore the church out of goodwill? Or has the church often given the world too little to reject, too little witness, too few challenges, a too small God and a harmless Jesus? This book shares the conviction

---

employ the language of the powers to condemn the Constantinian yoking of Christianity with the sword are not always clear on this point. Nevertheless, I believe their central insights are correct: the powers are fallen and so, while not necessarily coercive, they happen to be so; therefore Christendom is an idolatry (not necessarily but contingently—we might say it *has been* or *was* an idolatry; or, what is idolatrous is not necessarily identification with the state but the idea that God's power is insufficient apart from coercive power of any sort to accomplish God's ends).

of those who assert that it is the latter. The true church is still a martyr-church despite its relative shortage of martyrs. The relative shortage of martyrs does not *necessarily* mean anything, since martyrdom does not prove the church's faithfulness, the boldness of its witness, nor the righteousness of its cause. And yet God's promises to enlist the persecution inflicted on martyrs in extending the church's mission have real meaning and continuing relevance to the church insofar as it commits itself to bearing witness to a hostile world that nevertheless belongs to God.

The church's failure to be a martyr-church is supremely seen in those cultures that continue to baptize the young for sentimentality's sake. For many, baptism involves neither incorporation into the life of the community of faith nor incorporation into the death and resurrection of Christ. It is not a drowning in the surging waters, a participation in the suffering of Christ, a commitment to undergo the discipline of the church relative to its new life and mission made possible by Christ's resurrection. For many, baptism does not recall and invite the promises of God to the new member, those promises that will be necessary in a life marked by dedication and risk. Rather, it forgoes the weightier matters of life and death in favor of sanctioning the life and choices one will make on one's own. In absolute contrast to the gift God has given the church in baptism for marking the difficulty of discipleship and God's upholding, for many baptism only enshrines one's individual life apart from God and entrenches one's autonomous freedom from the church. It becomes a quaint ceremony for an innocuous blessing, a hopeful but ultimately bland sign for receiving good things from life, a plea for calm and good luck, a positive omen, and perhaps an exercise in superstition. What is certain is that many are baptized who have no intention of dying with Christ or suffering for their faith.

But just as baptism is a gift by God enriched with promise, the church must continue to trust that God will preserve its life for its gospel mission despite the way that that life appears to be undermined, in this case, from within. This is surely the more difficult of the challenges to the martyr-church: not persecution from the outside but weakening from the inside. It is tempted to think that its common life can be marked by the calm displayed by those who want the church but do not want to suffer because of it. It is asked to provide fellowship but not challenge. It is asked to provide blessing but not discipline. But is this not identical to the situation of the church in a world that only shows apathy to its existence? Is this not how the world co-opts the existence of the church to its own ends and for its own purposes? Indeed the very creation and existence of the church are beset by internal and external threats with much in common, not least of which is God's promise to create and uphold it despite these threats.

41

2

CARRYING CROSSES

E ven though baptism is a death, it is also just the beginning. Jesus's invitation does not stop with "Repent and be baptized" but persists through "Follow me." It is no small point that what it means to "follow" Jesus is categorically different from following Socrates or some other great teacher. In the latter instances, we assume the master would have his disciples follow his teaching and his way of life. Certainly this is true of Jesus's disciples as well. There is no further justification for why we ought to love our neighbors than that this is what Jesus taught. It is not necessary to provide a surer source of authority for welcoming children, showing mercy to strangers, or visiting the imprisoned other than that these are all part of what it means to follow Jesus's teaching. In these ways, a follower of Jesus is not distinct *in kind* from a follower of Socrates. Moreover, followers of both great men may adopt a different way of life

43

from that of others. They may ask challenging questions in the marketplace or denounce the powerful not only because they have been taught to do so but also, more importantly, because they follow a way of life from which such activities naturally proceed. It is common now to speak about philosophy itself as a way of life rather than a set of ideas, a description that surely accords with the Classical practice of following a master.

However, following Jesus departs from this in two significant ways. First, while the follower of Jesus seemingly obeys his teaching, she is actually found to be obeying a living person.[1] The words of Jesus do not constitute a body of knowledge or a comprehensive set of instructions, obedience to which is outlined in advance of the church's reception of it. Rather, as a living person, Jesus calls for present-day disciples to follow in an authority that, for us, is constituted by the resurrection.[2] In believing in the resurrection of Christ, the church affirms the continual presence of the Resurrected One to its life together. This means that, among other things, its reading of scripture is likewise guided by following. The church is entitled to a kind of "radical hermeneutics" with regard to its scriptures because it entrusts its reading of them to the life formed by the One who is its scriptures' central character. This is part of what is meant by the claim that scripture is a living word. In a

1. This is implied by Karl Barth's observation that the New Testament never uses the substantive word *discipleship*, meaning that the call to follow Jesus is always what Barth calls an "event" rather than a general concept. See *Church Dogmatics*, 4/2, trans. G. W. Bromiley et al. (Edinburgh: T & T Clark, 1956–75), 534.

2. David Clough has successfully defended Barth's ethics along these lines, arguing that a dialectical mode is necessary in order to avoid possessing Christ within a system. This means that any authentically Christian ethic is first a Christology. *Ethics in Crisis: Interpreting Barth's Ethics* (Aldershot, UK: Ashgate, 2005).

more christological key, the dwelling of the Word among us (John 1:14) has meant more than the delivery of law since, as the fulfillment of the law of Moses, Christ's living presence in the world constitutes an authority that is different in kind. In Mark, this sets Jesus apart from the teachers of the law at an early stage (1:22). The Law of Christ is no more fixed in stone than was his body kept back by a stone. Rolled away, that stone door liberated the living Christ to the world as the eternal law of God, not merely as once given but as continually present to the world as the living Word.

We might wonder if a living Jesus is not more than a little arbitrary, since we take comfort in those things that do not change. This points to the second aspect that makes following Jesus unique. The way of life Jesus sets forth is by means of leading the church in that way, not only by example but by promise. It is a way of life without prior guarantees that proceed from the past into the future. The choices it involves are not governed by changeless patterns and meta-level theorems. A God who is the same yesterday, today, and tomorrow is a relief in a world of shifting loyalties, unpredictable whims, and inconstant loves. But a God who goes before us and bids us follow into the unknown, with only the light of faith, is rather more disturbing. As with any law we are asked to follow, we would rather have prior assurances that the politics or economy of that law are stable, that they apply equally to everyone in the interest of justice, and that they somehow aim at the common good. However, the church of faith is granted no separate mitigation of the risk it is asked to take, nor is it given assurances that its following will achieve anything.

It is important to clear a space in this way for what needs to be said next regarding Jesus's call for disciples to take up crosses and follow him.

45

> If any man would come after me, let him deny himself
> and take up his cross and follow me. For whoever would
> save his life will lose it; and whoever loses his life for
> my sake and the gospel's will save it. For what does it
> profit a man, to gain the whole world and forfeit his life?
> For what can a man give in return for his life? (Mark
> 8:34–37)

It has been too common to misunderstand what taking
up "your cross" means, putting the emphasis on *your*
rather than *cross*. As a result, the crosses Christians have
understood themselves to be carrying are occasions of
suffering: a lost job, a lost child, a disability. My cross to
bear may be different from yours, and everyone needs to
discover what theirs is and then resolve to bear it without
too much grumbling. But this is a gross misunderstanding of Jesus's words.[3] It is not as though Christianity has
nothing to say to those who grieve and suffer loss, nor
that Jesus does not care, but this is simply not what is
meant by the call to carry crosses. Because following
Jesus is an unpredictable activity, assured only by trusting in promise, it cannot make reference to burdens that
are known quantities.

The key to understanding this command is the word
cross. It speaks of suffering as a convicted criminal and
of death at the hands of Romans. It makes clear reference to the opposition the Jesus movement would face,
to Jesus's determination that its members would stand
firm and be prepared to suffer the consequences of
being a part of it. These are not the consoling words of
a gentle pastor; they do not soothe or comfort those who
grieve. Rather, they resemble a rallying call spoken the
night before a final confrontation with the forces of the

3. Dietrich Bonhoeffer, *The Cost of Discipleship*, trans. R. H. Fuller (New
York: Touchstone, 1995), 88.

enemy. In fact, if it were any other political movement, we would be tempted to call it a call to arms. It is not a call *to arms*, but only because arms are precluded from playing a role in the revolution of the crosses. But it is no less a revolution for being nonviolent.

Users of violence have abandoned their crosses for more effective means of achieving results. This is why it is important to see that it is not only the crosses that refuse violence, suffering it rather than inflicting it, but also that following Jesus is not a means of achieving something. Because following Jesus is categorically different from following anybody else in that the risk of following cannot be mitigated by the actions of the followers, the logic of that following actually entails the refusal of violence. Put differently, a present-day follower of Gandhi is not guided by a present-day Gandhi but only by a historical body of teaching and technique. Given this, the teaching and technique become the tools of resistance but cannot be sufficient for making those who use them practitioners of nonviolence in the same way as those who bear crosses for the sake of a living guide. If following Jesus were like following Gandhi in this way, then the nonviolence inherent in bearing crosses rather than fighting in order to refuse them could be understood only with recourse to something other than Christian discipleship.

The church bears its cross when it does not ask what purpose the cross serves. It does not ask about whether it can better devote its energies to more worthwhile projects. It does not speculate about the relative goodness of Rome or whichever powers rule over it. If it did these things, it would only provide itself with reasons, with pros and cons. To these, it would then not only be able to invite counter-reasons but also court violence as a tool for change in its very deliberation to undergo the suffering involved, ironically, in its refusal to use violence. Christian crosses are not *reasons* to refuse violence. They are nothing less than the way the church refuses violence; they are themselves the church's refusal of violence. There are no counter-crosses, that is, ways of following Jesus apart from the risk of death at the hands of the powerful. There are only those who suffer violence and those who inflict it, those who hang on crosses and those who drive the nails. Christian peace is in the shape of a cross because it cannot be a way of avoiding violence but only a way of refusing it: refusing it by suffering it and suffering it for refusing it. Put simply, the church bears its cross for no other reason than that Jesus bore one first.

In turn, this forms the identity of the church. Mark makes clear that those who carry crosses do so unashamed of Jesus and the gospel.

> For whoever is ashamed of me and of my words in this adulterous and sinful generation, of him will the Son of man also be ashamed, when he comes in the glory of his Father with the holy angels. (8:38)

The suffering of the church for the sake of the gospel is not somehow proof that it is not ashamed. Rather, its suffering is its not-being-ashamed; it is how the church acts in solidarity with the cross of Christ. Again, it is important to emphasize that suffering does not authenticate the church's witness, nor does it substantiate its testimony. If it did these things, the church would be free to investigate other ways of authenticating and substantiating. Against this, bearing crosses is itself the witness of the church to the claim that Jesus is the Christ. In the next chapter it will be shown how Peter's confession, "You are the Christ," actually amounts to a denial in relation to this very point. It belies his unwillingness to take up his cross.

And, indeed, Jesus names our unwillingness in economic terms: "For what does it profit a man, to gain the whole world and forfeit his life?" (8:36). The "whole world" is the domain for the preaching of the gospel, the place where witnesses will make known the story of Jesus and his identity as the Christ (14:9). It should not be surprising that the "whole world" is also the source of temptation for Christians to abandon the suffering of the cross. Despite the economic language, this is not the whole world of bigger houses and swelling bank accounts which Christians ought to refuse for the sake of an ascetic ethic. It does not refer to the temptation toward greater wealth or a vast fortune that can overtake the good intentions of weak Christians. Rather, the whole world is those other "souls" to whom the gospel will be preached. It is the world outside the church, the ones who need to hear about new life in Christ. That world will hear about the loving act of anointing Jesus before burial done by a woman who knew that Jesus would die and yet did not abandon him. Instead, she did a "wonderful thing."

> And truly, I say to you, wherever the gospel is preached in the *whole world*, what she has done will be told in memory of her. (14:9, emphasis added)

The temptation named by gaining the whole world yet forfeiting one's life is the temptation to turn the gospel into a weapon (a weapon that the woman, for one, refuses). It is the temptation to make the gospel do something, to bend it to our purposes, rather than let the good news encounter the unbelieving world open to the possibility of rejection. The problem is that a gospel-weapon has only the appearance of the gospel. But like the invitation to take up crosses, the gospel for the whole world is extended as an invitation, an offer, and it refutes itself when the world is not free to reject it. Simon of Cyrene was forced to carry a cross, but not by Jesus. Christian disciples may also be forced to carry crosses, but only because they have already determined for themselves that this amounts to their discipleship as free creatures.

In the same way, the church remembers its martyrs freely, refusing to let its memory of them become an excuse for violence. Martyrs are those who are remembered by the church for having carried crosses to death, thereby sharing in the death of Christ. By remembering them in this way, the church does not embrace death so much as embrace as part of its ongoing life those who have died in the cause of Christ. A martyr-church remembers its fallen members as followers of Jesus.[4] Nevertheless, it is also appropriate that the church identify its martyrs as martyrs through a process of its life together. Whether its members are truly martyrs, and thus how they should be remembered, requires discernment.[5] This is a reminder that there are no self-proclaimed martyrs, a reminder that has two aspects.

First, just as it is not possible to become a member of the church by baptizing oneself, so also it is not possible

4. René Girard suggests that what distinguishes Christian martyrdom from other forms is that the Christian martyr does not die in order to be copied. See: Henri Tincq, "An Interview with René Girard," Le Monde, November 6, 2001. It is probably a mistake to generalize about all non-Christian martyrdom, but Girard is surely right that one who wants others to die too cannot be a Christian martyr.

5. Elizabeth A. Castelli documents how, in practice, the ways that martyrs are remembered are complex and sometimes unfortunately ideological. See Castelli, Martyrdom and Memory: Early Christian Culture Making (New York: Columbia University Press, 2004).

to become a martyr by directly seeking it or in some way killing oneself. Martyrdom is different from suicide. Seeking martyrdom is succumbing to the temptation to separate "take up your cross" from "follow me." It is the tendency to grasp at certainty, even of the meaning of one's own death, by calling it martyrdom. But martyrs entrust themselves to the church's memory with no guarantee that the church will discern the meaning of their death in its continued existence.[6] This is not because they might be betrayed by the church but because even in death they openly subject themselves to the church's discipline. After all, the way the church narrates the past is a work of disciplining its tendency toward self-deception and learning to speak truthfully, especially about those things at which it has failed. "For what credit is it, if when you do wrong and are beaten for it you take it patiently? But if when you do right and suffer for it you take it patiently, you have God's approval" (1 Pet. 2:20).

Second, the church proclaims its martyrs, the living on behalf of the dead. Its justification for doing so is the fact that Christ is risen and present in the church. The dead in Christ have been raised with him and are likewise still a part of the church. They still play a role in how the church makes decisions through their memories made

6. In a discussion of the "revolutionary suicides" of Jonestown, Stanley Hauerwas argues that they could not be martyrs precisely insofar as their suicide was meant to be revolutionary. See *Against the Nations: War and Survival in a Liberal Society* (Notre Dame, IN: University of Notre Dame Press, 1992), 102. In protesting a world that would not welcome the kind of community they wanted to create (that is, by trying to make a point about the world), the People's Temple could not escape the implication that their deaths became determined by the very world they opposed, making them victims of that world. There was no one left to discern the meaning of their would-be martyrdom, since there was no one to discern the truth or falsity of their life and witness.

present to us by the resurrection. Deciding to remember them as martyrs, therefore, is part of the church's work of memory. Martyrs are not self-proclaimed, because such a proclamation would be self-refuting. The proclamation of martyrdom by those about to undergo it themselves belies a separation from the church, a lack of faith in its collective memory that shows itself to be a lack of faith in the risen Christ's presence to the church. In short, self-proclaimed martyrs cannot believe in the resurrection, meaning that they cannot be martyrs.[7]

But the church does not remember only martyrs. Because of baptism, it must remember all of its members, as it does at the feast of All Saints'. Still, there is a particular challenge inherent in the question of how Christians ought to remember those whose use of violence has kept them from being celebrated as martyrs. Those who have died in battle are often spoken of as having given their life, but it would be a mistake to say that they have carried a cross. In Mark's narrative, there are actually no disciple-martyrs but only fighters and fleers. Those who fight are included with those who flee, since all are revealed to be deserters (see chapter 4). Neither fighters nor fleers are promised to be remembered as agents of Christ's peace to the nations. Instead, they represent a truncated version of true peace, expressed for fleeting periods as interludes within a more determinative warfare.[8]

7. I do not intend to engage the debate over the origins of the Christian understanding of martyrdom, though I am sympathetic with Daniel Boyarin's appeal for viewing martyrdom as a "discourse" rather than a single thing, such as a text's description of a violent death. See *Dying for God: Martyrdom and the Making of Christianity and Judaism* (Stanford, CA: Stanford University Press, 1999), 94. It would not be surprising to learn that Christians, in discerning how to remember their martyrs, found that martyrdom itself is not a simple concept.

8. There is an opposite danger of too readily invoking the description of martyrdom in application to those who neither fight nor flee. When this is

The assumption that peace is the absence of war enforces the logic of militarism and the force of nations, it underwrites the unending nature of worldly conflict in the name of ersatz peace, and it promises salvation on the foreshortened horizon of human history in which the primary actors wield military might. The idea that martyrs rather than soldiers truly hold the key to peace among the nations is so counterintuitive that it requires prophets to tell it to us, many of whom we have killed for it. Our killing of them did not keep them from coming, a fact that itself fulfills the promises made to all prophets who would speak the truth at great risk.[9] We have not been overpowered by prophets, persuasive in their coercion, but potentially underwhelmed by the generous offer of Christ, whose call goes forth in freedom to those who do not believe. It is already known that many will reject it, though those who accept can struggle with the world with no instrument more powerful than the weakness of Christ's cross. But when the message of the gospel is rejected, its rejection is often demonstrated in its infliction of violence on those who proclaim that violence has been rendered unnecessary.

---

done, as Castelli argues, violence and truth are coupled together and enshrined in the memory of the community that attaches the label *martyr* exactly to the extent that the truth of the martyr's witness is assured by their suffering of violence. Castelli discusses the hagiographic cult of martyrdom surrounding Cassie Bernall, who was killed at Columbine High School in 1999. Castelli worries that the ancient Christian martyr tradition recapitulates into contemporary examples like Bernall's an insistence that "death is a meaning-producing event, that truth and violence inexorably imply each other—and that, indeed, the first requires the second" (*Martyrdom and Memory*, 196). At the very least, this suggests that the association of violence and truth does not disappear when the dead are remembered as martyrs, for this may only prolong the inevitability of violence itself. We need only think of the suicide-bomber-as-martyr phenomenon.

9. See Mark 12:1–12, which will be discussed below.

The church cannot remember fighters as martyrs. Still, it may remember them *in light of* martyrs.[10] It may remember its failures to display the peace of Christ through its members to the world. The problem is severe where the church cannot call to mind any who have suffered with Christ in martyrdom even while it readily celebrates scores of fighters. But it is more severe still when it positively remembers those who have fought for nations as accomplishing the work of the gospel that only martyrs can do in their refusal to use force.

How shall we account for this? Later in Mark's Gospel, Jesus addresses his disciples with apocalyptic language that parallels the earlier call to take up crosses and details some features of what their resistance may entail: "Many will come in my name, saying, 'I am he!' and they will lead many astray. And when you hear of wars and rumors of wars, do not be alarmed; this must take place, but the end is not yet" (13:6–7). Though we hear of "wars and rumors of wars," we are told "But the end is not yet." When fighters are wrongly remembered as

10. Karl Rahner, appealing to Aquinas in the latter's commentary on the *Sentences*, thinks we ought to broaden our concept of martyrdom to include fighters who defend society against enemies of the faith. See Rahner, "Dimensions of Martyrdom: A Plea for the Broadening of a Classical Concept," in *Concilium*, ed. Johannes-Baptist Metz and Edward Schillebeeckx (Edinburgh: T & T Clark, 1983), 9–11. Rahner asks why Archbishop Oscar Romero, one who "fought" for justice, should not be a martyr. But Rahner must appeal to a strong binary abstraction of *active* and *passive* martyrdom in order to make his case, categories I suspect will not bear as much weight as he seems to hope. Moreover, it is far from being the case that the struggle for justice must be violent. In this way, William T. Cavanaugh's call for breaking down the separation between the "religious" and "political" implications of confessing Christ appeals to what is right about Rahner's concern (see Cavanaugh, *Torture and Eucharist* [Oxford: Blackwell, 1998], 62). Though it does not have an obvious answer, one is reminded of the question of whether Bonhoeffer is a martyr, on which see Craig J. Slane's thorough *Bonhoeffer as Martyr: Social Responsibility and Modern Christian Commitment* (Grand Rapids: Brazos, 2004).

martyrs, they function as heroes in a dangerously false gospel that declares that the "end" *is*, in fact, to be found in warfare and the proclamation of warfare. The duality in reference to wars and rumors of wars is a cipher where we find remonstrances of the messianic alternative of peace. Rumor is taken to be knowledge-bearing by those who have no reason to doubt the truth of the rumor. Still, the disciples are warned to be suspicious of such declarations, since they will involve false messiahs (13:6), and their ability to recognize and refuse the messages of false messiahs will be bound up with their ability to resist the temptation to believe that rumors of warfare signal the consummation of history. The problem, of course, is that we too readily believe that war is always somehow "the end" without recognizing that such speech is only characteristic of a demonically retrograde *polis* that the church refuses to adopt. Rumors of war declare that kingdoms and nations are falling and rising, bourgeoning and withering: the very actions that define those kingdoms as kingdoms. On such grounds, the *civitas terrena* is constantly renewed. The world is characterized by its ability to sustain rumors of wars, to keep them alive, not only as a way of sharing information but as a way of sharing beliefs and convictions about what is most central to its political identity.[11]

Jesus warns that despite wars and rumors of wars, the end is not yet. This is not the kind of prediction that speaks of the end and what it will be like; it is rather a warning that these are things we might otherwise associate with

11. As Gordon Allport and Leo Postman argue in *The Psychology of Rumor* (New York: Russell and Russell, 1965), rumor is not a private phenomenon; it requires that the plausibility structures for reception and transmission be shared. "Each rumor has its own public . . . which exists wherever there is a community of interest" (180). Similarly, see Jacques Ellul, *Propaganda: The Formation of Men's Attitudes* (New York: Vintage, 1973), 287–94.

55

the end but, in fact, they are still far from the end. If anything, they are the beginning of the end: "This is but the beginning of the birth-pangs" (13:8). This image trades, interestingly, not on endings but on beginnings, not the coming end of the final chapter but the start of the next one: the beginning of the birth-pangs is the start of something new. Indeed, the point of apocalyptic discourses like this is to give an indication of the nature (certainly not the *timing*) of the end. It locates the horizon of what is paradigmatically determinative for human and divine history by distinguishing the surd from the serious. The rumors of wars relate to this phase, which is passing away and threatens to suggest itself with finality. The warning for disciples is against believing in its finality. Jesus does not say what the end will be like, only that it will not be like *this*. Or, rather, here are some things that seem endlike, but they are not truly endlike. They only seem endlike because they reflect a posturing of false pretensions and surrogate determinances. The martyr-church is warned against anticipating the closure that warfare promises.

Jesus's witnesses proclaim the arrival of a kingdom that does not yet mean the destruction of enemy kings through war. This transmutes into two kinds of temptation. On the one hand is the temptation to believe that the kingdom is indeed the kind of kingdom brought by violence and so to hasten to bring it about through violent means, namely, crusades. On the other hand is the temptation to think that since the kingdom has not come with force, it has not actually come at all. The warning that the end is not yet is directed against this second temptation. The credulity offered to rumors of wars is from those who are beginning to despair of God's timing, the so-called delay of the parousia, the impatience for God's judgment to set the world right by bringing the kingdom of God in its fullness.

When it is present, the former temptation, that is, the temptation to bring in the kingdom by violent means, makes Jesus's words ironic. This is because his words are not so much ignored as put to use in popular literature and so-called prophetic sermons that take for their theme "rumors of the end" in the form of speculation about the proximate consummation of history. The point Jesus was making by warning that "the end is not yet" is therefore entirely overturned and, incredibly, made to sanction the perdurance of the very rumors that are sustained by the indiscernibility of the kingdom of God. When the kingdom is not plain, there is a danger that Christians will allow themselves to be fascinated by worldly ways of making things happen. Is this a heresy tantamount to the affirmation of a false messiah which Jesus condemns with the selfsame words, though it is ironically enlisted in defense of orthodoxy? Like idolatry in its most insidious form, the danger here is less a matter of premeditated worship of a messiah other than Christ and has more to do with an undue enchantment with another kind of would-be christological sovereignty.

How do we account for this irony? How is it that what is meant to postpone the end beyond the ultimacy of warfare can actually become the occasion for associating warfare with the end? There is a version of false messianism that unintentionally ascribes ultimacy to warfare since it suspects that it is actually locating it within peace. The false messiah brings deliverance, that is, peace, *through* war. The rumor spreads, not that wars have begun but that they are about to end. They are like the rumors of peace that circulated in late April and early May 1945, though the end of World War II was still to come.

It is important to see how the logic of the false messiah for those who have grown weary of war actually belongs to the same story about the world as does the false messiah of those who have not yet grown weary of war, particularly as war benefits them. There is a common assumption shared by those who need war to end as much as by those who need war to continue. This sounds unfair to those who suffer the ravages of war, but it only recalls for us that these are the ones who are most likely to believe that the end of war registers the coming of a kingdom of peace. This kind of false messianic hope is tied to the end of war on grounds that, ironically, makes impossible the end of *all* war but rather ensures its inevitability. Rumors of peace perpetuate on the same principle as rumors of war precisely because they both misplace instrumentality in worldly, noneschatological achievement. John Lennon's humanistic refrain that war will end "if you want it" is tempting for exactly this reason.

A messianic hope is not the generalized hope of everyone for deliverance but the vision that such a hope must take if it is to be a part of God's eschatological work. Likewise, when the apocalyptic voice announces that "he who endures to the end will be saved" (13:13), we can see that the forces that work to forestall this endurance are the forces that make rumors of wars, and so false messiahs, inevitable. The call is against the rumor-mill called "world" that anxiously passes on news from the frontlines; it is in favor of an ecclesiological patience that knows that those frontlines are not finally the locus for deciding the outcome of history. At issue is not the interminability of war and violence but their promise to save.

The discipleship of martyrs, therefore, is not marked by a resistance to grandiose, utopian wishes but by a resistance to too-small hopes. It is oriented toward the discipline necessary to resist rumors that are too easily believed. How is this discipline accomplished? Nietzsche famously took Christian morality to be based on a self-destructive asceticism.[12] At first glance, there would seem to be more than a suggestion of this in the call to "deny yourself." However, Nietzsche's problem was that he was unable to see what asceticism has to do with following. In Mark's Gospel, self-denial is the condition of possibility for following Jesus. *Askesis* (from which *asceticism* is derived) is a term that names the training or discipline of self-denial, though not as a good in itself. There is nothing inherently praiseworthy in actions that deprive one of the good life, pleasure, or joy. Rather, insofar as such actions enable one to live in preparedness and patience for the crisis that their following will entail, they are commendable actions. So long as being deprived of one thing assists the ability of obtaining something of surpassing quality or higher excellence, such deprivation is worth it. In the same way, *martyrdom* names not an ethic but an effect or outcome of the *askesis* of one's whole life, one's needs, and the way of life that would meet them.[13]

It is important that martyrdom is not at the far end of a continuum marked out by various degrees of self-denial. It is not asceticism to the extreme, penitence with greater intensity, the most uncomfortable hair shirt imaginable. Instead, "deny yourself" is related to "take up your cross and follow me" as means to end. The former is necessary to accomplish the latter. The way of Jesus

12. Friedrich Nietzsche, *On The Genealogy of Morality*, trans. Carol Diethe (Cambridge: Cambridge University Press, 1994), esp. essay 3.

13. *Askesis* is best rendered as "practice" or "training" and connects with self-denial only inasmuch as to train for something requires a singleness of focus that necessarily supplants other things. See Michel Foucault, *The History of Sexuality*, vol. 2, *The Use of Pleasure*, trans. Robert Hurley (New York: Vintage, 1990), 72–77, and Pierre Hadot, *Philosophy as a Way of Life: Spiritual Exercises from Socrates to Foucault*, trans. Michael Chase (Oxford: Blackwell, 1995).

requires the unseating of those modes of behavior, ways of life, desires, and thoughts that are conditioned on scales of self-preservation, self-protection, and security for one's life. The church upholds its commitment to the way of Jesus when it helps its members undergo the discipline necessary to resist the lure of wealth and cultivate the imagination required to reject vanity, the humility to ignore temptations to feed the acquisition of power, the patience to wait for justice when wronged, and the courage to withstand harm without the soothing consolation of revenge. The virtues necessary to be a martyr are no different from the virtues necessary to be a faithful Christian.[14] This means that martyrdom is not a special calling for a select few but the commitment of every Christian and the responsibility of every church.[15] Even though not every individual Christian will be killed, there is no way to distinguish those who will from those who will not. Even though not every Christian will be remembered as a martyr, every church that locates its identity in the cross is obligated to cultivate the virtues necessary to enable all of its members to die for the cause of Christ. Every Christian is a member of a martyr-church.

If self-denial does not *cause* martyrdom, it would be nevertheless misleading to deny that a martyr dies

14. Brad S. Gregory cites examples from the Middle Ages in which martyrdom supplies the language for expressing asceticism in its various forms. See Gregory, *Salvation at Stake: Christian Martyrdom in Early Modern Europe* (Cambridge, MA: Harvard University Press, 1999), 313.

15. Statements such as this ostensibly contradict Barth, who claims that "martyrdom or witness is an act which can be realized only on the basis of a special summons in a special situation" (*Church Dogmatics* 3/4, 79). Nevertheless, what makes martyrdom "special" for Barth is the fact that it is not sought rather than its being a vocation that requires a separate set of virtues. Therefore, I intend to agree with Barth while emphasizing a different point.

because his or her self-denial is extreme. After all, even though martyrdom is not an intrinsic good, it can still confirm that the self-denial that led to martyrdom was sufficient, that it was worth it. Such confirmation differs from proving that the martyr's testimony is true; in fact, confirmation occurs only in the minds of those who are likewise involved in the work of the disciplined body that produces martyrs in the first place. The church's ability to produce martyrs is confirmed by the actual deaths of martyrs. This is to say that the disciplined way of life made possible by the common life of worship, prayer, service, and ministry in the church identifies the intrinsic good of self-denial. The watchfulness of the disciples in the garden required the *askesis* of the body, not for its own sake but for the sake of prayer. The ability to pray to resist temptation was a function of disciplining the body, not first for the sake of resistance as such but for the specific act of prayer. In this way, self-denial is necessary for martyrdom, though it is precluded from being its efficient cause.

Similarly, self-denial does not kill the martyr. The martyr does not die of neglect or self-mastery, which we would more accurately speak of as suicide. Rather, self-denial enables the martyr to face with courage the situation that calls for death, though that death is inflicted by someone else. In this way, the martyr is freed from the necessity both of killing his accusers and of killing himself. Rejecting the necessity of both requires the kind of formation intrinsic to the *askesis* of a martyr-church, rejecting the offer to take control of the situation through violent means. The martyr exhibits confidence in peace as a powerless hope that is no less hopeful on account of being powerless, disabused of the means of securing life through coercion. The offer of Christ's peace cannot be safeguarded from rejection without imperiling its peaceableness. Those who bear crosses do so in the confidence that a new world has been created in which, despite appearances, the peace of Christ is a more sure reality than the violence of human agonism. The latter is a depleted shadow world that exists solely by reference to the cross. The church, therefore, does not simply witness to facts but displays the new life made possible by life in a new world set in motion by Christ himself. Its offer to the old world is animated only by its promise to persuade without coercion, in which martyrdom signals just how new the new world is since it does not rely on the abortive and evacuated promises of peace enshrined in the strategies of the old world.

3

BEHOLDİNG GLORY

The identity of Jesus is central to Mark's Gospel. From the beginning of his ministry when demons who speak it are silenced to the trial when the question is finally put to him by Pilate, the question of who Jesus is occupies a place of prime concern. Identity comes in the form of names and titles, and while Jesus's name is not in question, no doubt the meaning of the titles is. Even though Mark makes frustrating use of the obscure epithet "Son of Man," it is the deceptively more straightforward "Christ" that generates the most confusion at the midpoint of the Gospel.

In Mark, there are three major pronouncements of Jesus's identity. They come as a voice from heaven at the beginning of the story at Jesus's baptism (1:11), at the middle of the story at the transfiguration (9:7), and at the end by a Roman centurion at the foot of the cross (15:39). It is tempting to see Peter's confession at Caesarea Philippi as a true statement about Jesus's identity. He gives a seemingly correct answer, that Jesus is the Christ, the Messiah.

> And Jesus went on with his disciples, to the villages of Caesarea Philippi; and on the way he asked his disciples, "Who do men say that I am?" And they told him, "John the Baptist; and others say, Elijah; and others one of the prophets." And he asked them, "But who do you say that I am?" Peter answered him, "You are the Christ." And he charged them to tell no one about him. (8:27–30)

Here Peter correctly distinguishes himself from the tide of popular opinion that makes Jesus either a prophet, a cohort of John the Baptist's ministry, or Elijah himself. He does not shrink from the challenge of using a title that has not been used of Jesus before. Only Mark's readers are given advance notice in the book's title that this book concerns Jesus the Christ (1:1). Peter overcomes the fear that so often otherwise grips the disciples, rendering them silent, diverting their conversation to more mundane matters, keeping them from daring to ask questions of real importance. On these grounds, Peter's identification of Jesus seems quite commendable.[1]

Nevertheless, Peter's so-called confession, while technically correct, cannot really be considered to be a knowledgeable rendering of Jesus's identity. Peter speaks but is immediately silenced by Jesus: "And he charged them to tell no one about him" (8:30). His error is then demonstrated by the subsequent confrontation regarding the

---

1. Mark no doubt displays the irony that though Jesus is the Christ, he can be known as such only through following (as I argue below), while even what looks like following can become yet another way to take shortcuts. See Stanley Hauerwas, *The Peaceable Kingdom: A Primer in Christian Ethics* (Notre Dame, IN: University of Notre Dame Press, 1983), 74.

64

road Jesus must walk down if "you are the Christ" is to be a true statement. Peter wants the kingdom to come in victory without the suffering that characterizes it, distinguishing *this* kingdom from all other kingdoms.

Peter's words are more naturally associated with those of the unclean spirits: "And whenever the unclean spirits beheld him, they fell down before him and cried out, 'You are the Son of God'" (3:11). They "confess" Jesus as the Son of God. But in both cases, the unclean spirits and Peter receive no praise or congratulations for giving a right answer.[2] Instead, there is only the command of silence (3:12; 8:30). Likewise the confessions of both Peter and the unclean spirits are followed by invitations to disciples to ascend a mountain—the only times this happens in Mark (3:13; 9:2).

In spite of this, we still find ourselves congratulating Peter for his right answer. We love our words and are distrustful of silence, thinking that someone who lacks words lacks knowledge. How much worship is really pressure of speech, a way of seizing control by naming things? A presumptive confession betrays an anxiety that would forestall the requirements inherent in the object of confession. We speak too soon in order to evade the implications of what we say. Speaking can be a way of *just* speaking. Knowing who Jesus is takes more than using the right words to describe him. If Peter in a faithless moment can call Jesus "Christ" and unclean spirits call him "Son of God," it is not surprising that the meaning of the church's words cannot exhaust what it means by using them. There is more to the claims of Jesus's identity than names and titles, since their meanings are bound up with the way the church puts them to use in the total context of

2. Peter is congratulated in Matthew.

65

Christian life and churchly existence. Peter's blocking of Jesus on the road names the desire to consume the benefits of the kingdom without engaging in the costs of discipleship.

This is why the identity of the church is bound up with the identity of Jesus.[3] The church is not a community that has *decided* to call God's Son by his true name and true identity. Its very existence owes to the identity of the Son of the Father who creates the world and the church through speaking in the Spirit. The church does not preexist its confession, since it is constituted by the truth of what it confesses—not only through the truth of words but insofar as those words are spoken truthfully. True confession is spoken by those whose very ability to utter it is identical with their ability to name their own existence as church.

Bizarrely, perhaps, this means that despite the debates as to Jesus's identity, it was actually *Peter's* identity that is thrown into question when he opposes Jesus on the road. On the one hand, Peter cannot at that moment be identified as a disciple. Because a disciple follows, those who can claim that identity are seen by Jesus when he looks over his shoulder behind him.

> And he began to teach them that the Son of man must suffer many things, and be rejected by the elders and the chief priests and the scribes, and be killed, and after three days rise again. And he said this plainly. And Peter took him, and began to rebuke him. But turning and seeing his disciples, he rebuked Peter, and said, "Get

---

3. Similarly, Hans Urs von Balthasar, in *A Theology of History* (San Francisco: Ignatius, 1994), describes how the statements Jesus makes about himself "are never an attempt to define the peculiar character of what he is, but are one and all meant to serve his mission" (32). We would expect that this would have an ecclesial dimension, since the constitution of the church according to the confession of his identity is part of Jesus's mission.

behind me, Satan! For you are not on the side of God, but of men." (8:31–33)

As he stands in front of Jesus, Peter's confession is shown to issue from one who cannot endure the meaning of his own words.[4] But this is more than a single disciple's misstep. It is a warning that Peter's otherwise orthodox confession actually places him outside the church.

On the other hand, Peter at that moment could not even properly be identified as Peter. Earlier, Jesus had given Simon his new name, Peter, just following the "confession" of the unclean spirits (3:16), perhaps relating the identity of Jesus to the new identities of his disciples. They were singled out as his, as having been granted a new kind of authority. But on the road, it seems that Peter's name no longer applies to him. As with the unclean spirits, Peter's identity at this point ceases to be related to the content of his confession. This means not only that we are wrong to call his words "confession" but that we should not refer to the speaker of them as Peter! The identity of the one who dares to speak the truth about God, and of his Son, comes into question since there is no neutral place to stand from which to offer ideas about who Jesus is. The question is not so much who Jesus is as who *we* are who call him Messiah and Lord. Therefore, it should not be surprising that Jesus associates Peter's identity with the opposition. "Get behind me, Satan," is as much a rebuke of Peter for having stepped in front of Jesus as it is an answer to Peter's unspoken challenge, "And who do *you* say that *I* am?" It should not be surprising that the

---

4. This account of Peter's confession partly follows Christopher Burdon, *Stumbling on God: Faith and Vision through Mark's Gospel* (Grand Rapids: Eerdmans, 1990). My reading of Mark's Gospel owes much to Burdon's tremendous book.

speaker of a truncated "confession" is associated with the unclean spirits.

Therefore, the second of the major pronouncements of Jesus's identity in Mark cannot be said to come from Peter. Instead, it comes from the cloud atop the mountain Jesus ascends six days later. "And a cloud overshadowed them, and a voice came out of the cloud, 'This is my beloved Son; listen to him'" (9:7). In contrast to Peter's words, the witness of the Father to the Son is true, because the Father knows the identity of the Son and their mutual identities are upheld by each other's faithfulness. Peter was unable or unwilling to be faithful to the identity of "Christ," a fact that made his confession actually a denial.

All three pronouncements are connected with the death of Jesus. In chapter 1 we saw the decidedly deadly character of baptism that surges in the drowning waters, though it was misunderstood by James and John as a power-granting rite. Only near the end of the story is the real meaning of Jesus's baptism displayed, in the words of a centurion: "Truly this man was the Son of God!" (15:39). Until then, the truthful confessions about Jesus's identity as the Son of God come from heaven itself. Until then, it seems, only the Father can speak about the identity of the Son in truth, for apart from the full revelation of the Son in glory, it is impossible or perhaps simply unlikely that he will be known as the Son. The glory of the transfiguration is of an apparently unmistakable kind, though it points beyond itself to the cross, which is simultaneously the unexpected site of glory and also so evident that even an enemy centurion cannot deny it.[5] Like so many other confessions, the centurion's is incomplete and spoken without understanding.

5. The transfiguration does not differ from the resurrection in the sense that, as Rowan Williams observes, "when the risen Christ is finally recognized,

It is tempting to see the transfiguration of Jesus as foreshadowing only the resurrection rather than the cross itself. To be sure, a transfigured Christ looks a lot like how we imagine a resurrected Christ. But apart from dangerously separating the cross and the resurrection, as will be shown below, this also reflects our desire to jump too quickly to the end of the story. Moreover, doing so violates Mark's purpose, exposing our penchant for triumph and power. Because, like Peter, we would rather have the glory of the kingdom without the suffering of the King, we would also rather have the resurrection without the cross. The problem is not that we see the kingdom in the resurrection or that we are wrong to look for the glory of the King. Instead, the problem is that we fail to see the kingdom come in the suffering of the King. Wanting a ruler other than the Suffering Servant, we mistake his coronation for his dethronement. This suggests that the church deserves its kings. Just as Israel was shown to deserve the tyrannous Saul, wanting to be like the other nations in respect of having a king, so also the church is left to its kings of national pride and process—its congressional representatives, its prime ministers, its presidents—when it has forgotten how to see that the kingdom of God has come in the form of a suffering servant. Insofar as the church contents itself with the reduced horizons and abortive expectations necessary to hope in the salvation of the nations by their leaders, it has already chosen its kings.

In contrast, the transfiguration is the site where the King is revealed as a servant. It is a vision of the

---

it is of course *as* the crucified." See Williams, *Resurrection: Interpreting the Easter Gospel* (London: Darton, Longman and Todd, 2002), 79. Put in the language used here, the resurrection and the transfiguration are both glorious precisely by displaying the identity of Jesus as the crucified one. Thus an inability to see one is bound up with an inability to see the other.

resurrection only so long as we are possessed of the kind of glory that follows the triumph of battle. It bespeaks victory too easily if it trades on images of those whose winning is made plain and obvious. But a transfigured Christ is not a resurrected Christ in any immediate sense. Instead, the glory of the transfiguration is the glory of the cross. The white robes of splendor are the reality of the bloody garments of the crucified. These robes do not become white by washing *away* the blood but by washing them *in* the blood. They are whiter than any soap can make them: "his garments became glistening, intensely white, as no fuller on earth could bleach them" (9:3). This is not a quaint reference to the relative ineffectiveness of earth's detergents but an indication that the garments have undergone an entirely different kind of washing. They are not white for being clean but for being righteous. They are not bleached but drenched.[6]

This is admittedly a terrible kind of glory. The cross is not a skirmish on the way to victory or an unfortunate death in a winning battle. It is the reorientation of the logic of battle itself. The terror of defeat is real—done away with not by what comes next but exactly by what it means for "terror" and "defeat." When the church awaits the coming of the kingdom "with power" only by looking forward, it fails to see that that power has already come.[7] The reason it is so difficult to see is that it looks like anything but power. We are removed from it not by distance but by sin and unbelief. Our ideas about where power is to be found are exposed as false. We fail to grasp the coming of the kingdom, not because it is so big but

6. Revelation 7:14: "They have washed their robes and made them white in the blood of the Lamb." See also Ched Myers's discussion of Jesus's garment in *Binding the Strong Man: A Political Reading of Mark's Story of Jesus* (Maryknoll, NY: Orbis, 1988), 250.

7. As Jesus remarks in 9:1.

70

because it is so small that it slips through our fingers (indeed, as a mustard seed, 4:30–32). It does not look like intensely glistening glory, white robes, and voices from heaven. Instead, it looks embarrassingly ordinary.

But this is not to say that the transfiguration has nothing to do with the resurrection. In fact, it clarifies that the resurrection cannot be understood without the cross.[8] The identity of the resurrected One, like the identity of the transfigured One, is each of these things only on account of the relation to the crucified One, not vice versa. "Listen to him" is followed by the silence of the cloud and the absence of Jesus's interlocutors because the words of Jesus to which the disciples were to listen had already come in his earlier description of suffering and his call to take up crosses.

> And a cloud overshadowed them, and a voice came out of the cloud, "This is my beloved Son; listen to him." And suddenly looking around they no longer saw any one with them but Jesus only. And as they were coming down the mountain, he charged them to tell no one what they had seen, until the Son of man should have risen from the dead. (9:7–9)

That the disciples ought to listen is not so much a commendation as a rebuke. Their failure to pay attention to the identity seemingly expressed by Peter's confession is bound up with their failure to see Jesus for who he is. Transfiguration is as much about voices as about visions, sounds as much as sights: seeing Jesus glorified and hearing the content of that glory.

8. Myers observes that "this vision is not itself to be the subject of 'proclamation' (cf. 5:16), for the disciples will not understand *its* meaning until they have understood the meaning of 'resurrection'" (*Binding the Strong Man*, 252).

It is important that Mark draws a parallel between Peter's words and the words from the cloud. Both address Jesus's identity, both sound correct to us, and both are followed by Jesus's telling the disciples with him not to tell anyone else about it. But this is where the similarities stop. Jesus prevents loose-lipped disciples from going around announcing that Jesus is the Messiah, unaware of what they are saying. But when he prevents them from speaking about what they have seen on top of the mountain, it is not clear that they would have known how to put it into words to begin with. They cower in fear, and the words they *do* speak—and it is Peter again who speaks—are clearly not adequate to the situation.

> And Peter said to Jesus, "Master, it is well that we are here; let us make three booths, one for you and one for Moses and one for Elijah." For he did not know what to say, for they were exceedingly afraid. (9:5–6)

The abundance of meaning in the transfiguration defies the work that words are meant to do. Just as we are tempted to control objects by naming them, so also an event that so radically violates expectations cannot be spoken of without doing violence to it.

It is to the credit of Christian tradition that it has never named the transfiguration except by this very mysterious word. The event can only be described but not explained. As the reference to the transfiguration in 2 Peter makes clear, the revelation of the glory of God has no meaning beyond itself; it offers no explanation and resists attempts to render it explicable (2 Pet. 1:16–18). It can be attested and witnessed to but cannot be captured by any discourse. There is not a body of knowledge to which the transfiguration refers, since its depths are not exhausted by epistemology.

The silence following Peter's confession is categorically different from the silence following the transfiguration. The former is the silence of rebuke; the latter is the silence of wonder. On the road, Peter is silenced for speaking too soon, too freely. But as he, James, and John descend from the mountain, they fear the inadequacy of their own speech. Even though they are instructed not to talk about what they saw "until the Son of man should have risen from the dead," it is not the instruction that keeps them in silence. Instead, the disciples are simply at a loss for words. They do not understand what rising from the dead means; they cannot explain what they just saw. Even though the New Testament clearly affirms the resurrection, it never tries to explain what a resurrection is. Even after Jesus's resurrection took place, it seems all the church could do was narrate it and inhabit the way of life it made possible.

But as we will see later, the ending of Mark issues a disturbing caveat to this. Fleeing the empty tomb, the women "said nothing to any one, for they were afraid" (16:8). Their silence, like the silence of the three disciples on the mountain, is marked by fear and confusion. The church is in the position of the women at the tomb, being told, "Go, tell." But it is not relieved of confusion by being told the meaning of the resurrection. Just as the disciples come down off the mountain, being told that their silence must be temporary, we know that it must not be broken prematurely in an attempt to name, grasp, and explain. The fear of the women issued in silence because they could not imagine speaking about something that they could not explain. In this way, the church learns that its duty in mission is narration and how to distinguish narration from explanation.

There are two reasons that narration is more appropriate to the glory of God than is explanation. First, *explanation* suggests too great a confidence in the powers of interpretation. We want to be able to know what something means because "what something means" is narcissistically taken to include only those things that are about us. Admitting a fullness of meaning that extends beyond our capacity of interpretation requires admitting that there are questions for which we do not have the answers. The glory of God does not exist or shine for our benefit. There is no necessary connection between God's glory and our function as its audience.[9] But explanation either rebuffs the excess questions or denies that they have any importance. Any explanation would be limited by the terms employed, the grounds for "making sense" of such an extraordinary event that challenges the very abilities of words. It is difficult to imagine how an *explained* transfiguration might issue for others in the same fear that gripped the disciples. *Telling* the story, however, invites those who were not present to enter the mystery and inhabit the story themselves, becoming characters in it.

The second reason that narration is more appropriate than explanation is that explaining the event makes the event itself replaceable, at least in principle. It suggests that what is conveyed by the appearance of God's glory might be conveyed by something else. It also suggests that what is conveyed is better than that which conveys it. This lowers the glory of God onto an epistemological horizon on which sit all other means of knowing and discovery.[10]

9. Indeed, just as God did not need to create, so also his glory does not depend on creation. I suspect that, together, these are two complementary reasons we may speak of creation as declaring the glory of God—that is, it does so freely and so (and only so) does it participate in such glory nonnecessarily.

10. John Milbank's discussion of narration and explanation in Paul Ricoeur is helpful. See *Theology and Social Theory: Beyond Secular Reason* (Oxford:

For example, if the glory of God explains that God is great, we will believe in God's greatness rather than face his glory. If it explains Jesus's authority, we will know he is authoritative, but we still may not "listen to him." It is not sufficient to think that the "point" of the transfiguration is the delivery of information, nor that it is the impartation of new knowledge. Yet there is a great temptation to imagine the disciples as the recipients of an esoteric insight or privy knowledge, able to pass on an explanation that might exist on its own, apart from those who have witnessed the glory of the Lord. This is the heresy of gnosticism: salvation without following, knowledge without witness. In contrast, Jesus was transfigured not to make a point but to make three disciples into witnesses. In 2 Peter, the point is explicitly made that it was not information that was passed to the churches by the apostles ("cleverly devised myths," 1:16), but the very power and presence of Jesus Christ on account of their having been eyewitnesses to his glory. Eyewitnesses, of course, when they speak about what they have seen, become narrators.

In addition to distinguishing between narration and explanation, it is important to understand the importance of an eyewitness account. If eyewitnesses become narrators, this is only because they cannot make appeals to more generally understood categories. They tell a story precisely because they cannot anchor the meaning of what they saw in universal laws of nature, ordinary human behavior, or the standard flow of historical events. This sets the eyewitness apart from the two other kinds of witness in the juridical idiom: character and expert witness.

Blackwell, 1990), 267. However, I worry that Milbank now no longer prioritizes narration as he once did.

A character witness sets the event in question within a larger framework. When an event is contested, this kind of witness is valuable for deciding if this is the sort of thing the accused person would have done given a whole host of other things he has done. The character witness does not know about the specific case at hand (the murder, the forged will, the shoplifting) as the eyewitness does, but he does know crucially about who is purported to have been involved in it. However, it is impossible for knowledge of the transfiguration of Jesus to be had by this kind of witness. Jesus's identity is the very thing that is called into question and that is therefore being clarified and revealed. Ironically, a character witness to the transfiguration would not have needed the transfiguration. If Jesus had been apprehended as the Suffering Servant rather than misunderstood under the ostensibly accurate title "Christ," then the glory of the Lord might have been withheld—but only because it would already have been beheld. Jesus would not have needed to be seen in the full glory of the Son with the Father, with Moses and Elijah, if he had already been "seen" clearly as the Son of the Father of the law and the prophets.

There is also the expert witness. If the eyewitness knows about the particular case and the character witness knows about the person, the expert witness knows neither of these things. Instead, she knows how cases like this one usually work—whether this kind of gun could have made that kind of bullet hole, whether this kind of medication could have had that kind of effect, whether this kind of act could be attributable to that kind of mental lapse. But just as the character witness is confounded by the identity of Jesus, so also the expert witness is immaterial, for Jesus's uniqueness admits of no general appraisal. In perfect freedom from established

76

ranks and divisions, Jesus will not be understood as a particular instance of something else. As Thomas Aquinas liked to point out, God is not a genus. Jesus is a one-off. In the transfiguration, the Son is revealed as the Son of the Father, a relationship that can be theorized about under the heading of Trinity, but not something that results from theory. Instead, it is known only by glistening robes and voices coming from clouds. No one is an expert on these things, since they do not refer back to a more definitive body of knowledge, a more basic theory, or a more axiomatic truth.

There is no expert substitute for seeing. The eyewitness is valuable for reporting particulars (did you hear one gunshot or two?), while the expert witness helps to make sense of those particulars (two shots are impossible from this kind of gun, meaning there were either two guns or the eyewitness misheard). But "making sense" is the temptation for an abortive witness that wants general expertise more than particular knowledge.

Nevertheless, not having seen in the same way the apostles did, the church is in a curious position relative to its confession of Jesus as the Christ. That the church has so prized the authority of the eyewitnesses is not a testament to its skepticism but a way of affirming that Christian faith is historic. It again suggests that the gospel is more than a set of eternal truths, that Jesus is not a symbol of a more fundamental reality. The suffering of Jesus resists being construed in general terms as, for example, a symbol of human suffering, pain, and solidarity.

Even so, it is wrong to think that the cross has *nothing* to do with human suffering, pain, and solidarity. It simply is not an instance of these concepts understood on grounds prior to and apart from the cross itself. The cross changes the meaning of suffering rather than only

being an example of it. In the same way, the transfiguration, as a vision of the cross, does not "tell us" that the
cross is the height of the Son's glory. Instead, it reframes
the question "What is glory?" In a word, it transforms.
It does not cause human pain to cease, but it promises
that the meaning of pain will not be exhaustively determined by those who inflict it. It captures the creativity
of suffering within the life and death of the Servant who
suffers out of love for the world and obedience to the
Father. It reveals that creation was not completed in the
distant past but continues in the redemption of what we
call natural and what God still calls good.

The death of martyrs is located here. When scholars
debate whether or not Jesus was himself a martyr, it is
necessary to answer no if it is assumed that *martyr* names
a univocal category, the meaning of which is obvious and
the content of which is understood ahead of the witness
of the three disciples. As such, it is not possible to identify
Jesus as an *example* of a martyr, a concept that admits
of a host of other exemplars.[11] This construes the work
of the cross according to a moral teaching such as fully
submitting to the consequences of our beliefs or holding
on to our beliefs at all costs, but it makes two mistakes
in doing so. First, it leaves the concept of martyrdom
to a realm of discourse that exists quite apart from the
content of the convictions for which the martyr suffers.
This is the mistake of separating the form from the content of the convictions. The point of praise becomes *that*
the martyr dies, remembered by those who share the
same convictions as the martyr. In the life of the church,

11. Because he accepts a prior definition of martyrdom, Lacey Baldwin
Smith is led to conclude that the resurrection of Jesus adds a "somewhat
unfair" element to the notion of martyrdom. See his *Fools, Martyrs, Traitors:
The Story of Martyrdom in the Western World* (New York: Alfred A. Knopf,
1997), 71.

this mistake is seen when Christians separate the work of Christ in the cross and resurrection from his life, teaching, and ministry. This is the oft-noted wedge that is dangerously driven between the Jesus who preached good news to the poor and the Jesus who saves souls. Affirming the martyrdom of Jesus as exemplary *as martyrdom* can, in this way, substitute for identifying the continuity between Jesus's life and death.

Second, when the cross is construed as moral teaching about holding fast to beliefs, this assumes that others who suffer and die for the same beliefs are also martyrs in the same way as Jesus. This makes Jesus one among many Christian disciples, though he may be seen as the first, most important, and most notable of them all. It assumes that the deaths of all subsequent martyrs are like Jesus's death in that they die for their convictions like he did, though they might also think that they "die for him"—understood as dying on behalf of or because of him. This mistakes how martyrs share in the death of Christ and makes of the church a body of mere memory that holds on to the heroic feats of the past, though at a safe distance. It extends the past into the present only superficially, since its ability to do so barely depends on the participation of the present faithful in the life of its collective memory. Against this, the life of the church lived in constant participation of the death of Christ produces a martyr-church. It shares in the death of Christ through baptism and renews this when it breaks bread. It admits the paradoxes of its own existence: its life is death-made, the bread it breaks is infinitely creative. It affirms that Jesus cannot be the first Christian martyr, since there are no Christian martyrs except those who die the death of Christ.[12]

12. For an insightful discussion of Jesus as a martyr, though along very different lines, see Gerald O'Collins, S.J., *The Calvary Christ* (Philadelphia: Westminster Press, 1977), chap. 1.

For these reasons, when scholars ask whether Jesus was a martyr, the answer must be yes if the church, as it should, allows itself to recognize Jesus in its martyrs. It will do so insofar as it takes its cues for what constitutes martyrdom from Jesus himself rather than from a prior understanding of what it is to die for something.[13] Jesus is clothed as the martyred churches of Revelation, but not because white is the color all martyrs wear, having been washed in the blood of their death. Rather, taking its cues from the cross of Christ, the church's martyrs wear white because their deaths share in the death of Jesus; their blood is shed as the very blood of Jesus himself. Jesus is not one martyr among many, the first in a long line of Christian martyrs, but martyrdom's very condition of possibility. Therefore, denying that Jesus is a martyr would lead to the unbearable conclusion that all other Christian martyrs die their own deaths, in their own blood, and only "because of" Jesus.

Identifying Jesus as the Christ cannot be separated from the kind of life and death he would experience. Martyrs are among those who know what it means to use this title to describe Jesus, since their own deaths are spoken of as corresponding *mutatis mutandis* with his. This is to say that martyr-deaths have no meaning when the meaning of Christ is lost, even by those who claim to be Christian.

---

13. See Leonardo Boff, "Martyrdom: An Attempt at Systematic Reflection," in *Concilium*, ed. Johannes-Baptist Metz and Edward Schillebeeckx (Edinburgh: T & T Clark, 1983), 12–13.

4

FLEEING THE CROSS

If the transfiguration was meant to clarify the identity of Jesus and the cross as the site of glory, the disciples' fleeing in the garden demonstrates how much this was misunderstood. When the disciples flee at Gethsemane, they demonstrate their unwillingness to follow Jesus to the cross.

This event follows directly after the Last Supper. Even though they all had shared in the cup, the blood of the covenant, they failed to drink deeply. They failed to share in the cup that Jesus prayed would be taken from him in the garden, the cup of suffering and death. They failed to see how the two cups are really the same: the cup of fellowship means fellowship in the martyr-church, the broken body of Christ; the cup of glory is the cup of shame; the cup of salvation is the cup of death. When confronted with the opportunity to lose their lives in the promise of gaining them back again, they choose to secure their own fate on their own terms and cease following Jesus to the cross.

> And as they were eating, he took bread, and blessed, and broke it, and gave it to them, and said, "Take; this is my body." And he took a cup, and when he had given thanks he gave it to them, and they all drank of it. And he said to them, "This is my blood of the covenant, which is poured out for many. Truly, I say to you, I shall not drink again of the fruit of the vine until that day when I drink it new in the kingdom of God." And when they had sung a hymn, they went out to the Mount of Olives. And Jesus said to them, "You will all fall away; for it is written, 'I will strike the shepherd, and the sheep will be scattered.' But after I am raised up, I will go before you to Galilee." Peter said to him, "Even though they all fall away, I will not." And Jesus said to him, "Truly, I say to you, this very night, before the cock crows twice, you will deny me three times." But he said vehemently, "If I must die with you, I will not deny you." And they all said the same. And they went to a place which was called Gethsemane. (14:22–32)

Until the garden, following meant walking the road to Jerusalem behind the guide. So long as the guide led under his own power, even though disciples might be confused, they nevertheless could follow with a certain amount of confidence. The road leads somewhere, to a goal that is distant but, we assume, worth the wait. What the disciples could not countenance, however, was that such following was preparation for the time when the guide ceased to lead under his own power. They could not understand that the road continued to lead from the garden to the cross. They could not envision that "follow me" is a constant call that applies even more poignantly at night, in the garden, when the security forces surround them.

It is worth asking what the disciples should have done when the crowd came to arrest Jesus. How should they have responded in obedience and friendship to Jesus? It seems that the disciples perceived two possibilities: fight or flee. The fighting response is most obviously displayed by the bystander who cuts off the ear of a slave of the high priest.

> But one of those who stood by drew his sword, and struck the slave of the high priest and cut off his ear. (14:47)

This event represents the more general temptation to rescue Jesus, to protect him from harm by using violence. It is repeated in the church's attempts to secure the justice of God apart from the actions of God, which it does when it mistakes the sufficiency of God's vengeance. If ever there was a reason to fight, surely it would be for the sake of Jesus, to spare him from injustice, defend his honor, defeat his enemies. Not only is this the justification for crusade, for taking up arms against one's opponents in the name of God's cause, but it is also often the religious rationale for warfare of any sort. Protecting the innocent other seems commendable and required on account of Christian love and justice. Intervening when someone is wrongly accused occurs to us as an obvious obligation for those who have learned to love God's creation, to call it good, and to seek righteousness. Fighting seems to be requisite not only according to our status as human but even more so for Christians.

This makes it all the more frightening to discover that only those who are *not* following Jesus to the cross are actually in a position to rescue him. Only those for whom violence is a means to a good end can imagine a fate for Jesus that is better than the suffering of the servant of God. Only those who carry swords are in a position

83

to use them. But the sword-bearers in Mark are not Jesus's disciples. They are the security forces and arresting crowd (14:43). The identity of the ambiguous figure who cuts off an ear is not revealed to readers of Mark as it is to readers of John. He does not clearly emerge from either the crowd or the gathered disciples. Rather, he opposes equally both Jesus and the crowd. He strikes at the arresting crowd, making his opposition to the security forces obvious enough. But he also opposes Jesus in a sense. He contradicts the nonviolence of Jesus, who could have easily been arrested in the light of day while teaching in the temple. The night's darkness covers his actions to the same extent as his enemies'.

The disciples themselves failed to prepare in the garden by praying. If they had prayed as Jesus did, they would have responded to the arrest as he did, not by fighting nor by fleeing but by taking up crosses and following Jesus.[1] Those who had seen the radiant garments of the transfigured one were not prepared to wear those same robes. Just as they had misperceived the fate of Elijah in the death of John the Baptist on account of John's execution—for Elijah was not supposed to die—so also they misidentified the crisis of the Son of Man on account of Jesus's arrest. The link between arrest and cross is only too plain; it is the link between arrest and glory that is incomprehensible to minds that cannot see that the cross equals glory. Still, for such minds prayer is not necessary, since hearts are not troubled nor does temptation seem a problem.[2]

1. Rowan Williams insightfully sees that by refusing to fight or to flee, the disciple is actually more at home in the world than others, a comportment that is threatening to the world's systems of power, since it refuses to legitimate the ways that such systems establish themselves by way of violence and fear. See Williams, *Christ on Trial: How the Gospel Unsettles Our Judgement* (Grand Rapids: Eerdmans, 2003), 111.

2. It may not be a coincidence that the transfiguration is followed by another case of the disciples' failure to pray (Mark 9:29).

In light of this, it is important to understand why fighting was out of the question. It was not only because Jesus had to be crucified as part of God's plan. Rather, fighting is not the way of Jesus nor what he expects of disciples. Nevertheless, it is tempting for us to assume that Jesus is a special case, and while it might have been wrong to fight in his defense, this actually tells us nothing about whether we ought to fight to defend others. We assume that Jesus had to die but no one else does, that the Son's obedience to the Father occupies a realm of actions separate from the actions of those who have been made sons and daughters of God through adoption. Jesus's nonviolence was a function of his mission but did not constitute an ethic. There are two problems with this.[3]

First, it assumes that Jesus does not actually expect Christians to follow his example. Some theologians have notoriously made Jesus into less than the Son of God, a mere moral teacher. But assuming that he does not expect his followers to imitate his example makes him less than this still. When the metaphysical uniqueness of Jesus becomes the rationale for his being bound to a separate ethic, it is not the divinity of Christ but his humanity that is compromised. Jesus gets represented as more than human, as superhuman. This is the heresy of docetism in a moral mode. But the New Testament affirms the basis of Christian love to be the example of Christ precisely in respect of his refusal to let his metaphysical uniqueness entitle him to special privileges (Phil. 2). His extraordinary being is made ordinary entirely so that his life might be a human one, *not*

3. This question is taken up with extraordinary lyrical power by Dietrich Bonhoeffer in *The Cost of Discipleship*, translated by R. H. Fuller (New York: Touchstone, 1995), 86–101.

marked by an extraordinary ethical agenda, governed by inimitable moral principles, held to unprecedented inhuman achievements. Christians have to love each other *because* Christ became a servant, not despite the fact. Humility is a form of imitation. Likewise, the New Testament also affirms that the suffering of Jesus is both "for you" and an example to be followed.

> For to this you have been called, because Christ also suffered for you, leaving you an example, that you should follow in his steps. He committed no sin; no guile was found on his lips. When he was reviled, he did not revile in return; when he suffered, he did not threaten; but he trusted to him who judges justly. (1 Pet. 2:21–23)

When Jesus did not resist arrest, it was not only because he was an exceptional case in a plan that needed to be carried out for the sake of the world. This may well be true, but it risks misconstruing whether and how it impacts the Christian life. We may be led into thinking that the example of Jesus is irrelevant to the Christian life when we think that he is an exception to the normative behavior Christians are meant to exhibit. It is also true that had Jesus resisted his arrest, he might have evaded the cross and this to our peril. However, not only is this perceived as a travesty according to the logic that says that the cross had to happen, but, more important perhaps, an evaded cross is simply not God's way. The Son obeyed the Father to the point of death because he loves the Father as Son and therefore resembles the Father in faithfulness, not because he was bound to execute a separate and sufficient arrangement for a preset course of events.

Second, if Jesus is an exception in that fighting is suspended only for him, Christian martyrdom is an impossibility. Instead, Christians who die because they follow Jesus's example in not resisting would need to be remembered by the church as its fools, wide-eyed, quixotic dreamers who naively and unfortunately took the words of Jesus too literally. Rather than being witnesses to the gospel of Christ, they would be witnesses only of themselves. In the same way, Christians who die because of the hatred of the world to their witness could not be spoken of as participating in the death of Christ, because insofar as Christ is an exception, his death does not admit of this possibility. If the cross is a solitary event, given meaning only through the outworking of a plan for and by one extraordinary man, there could be no other crosses to bear. This leads to the unbearable implication noted before: that martyrs die their own deaths, isolated from the wounds and suffering of Christ.

In the end, however, all of the disciples flee the scene. It does not become the site of insurrectionist violence that both sides may have feared. Instead, after a brief scuffle, there is empty space, the disciples having gone one way and the arresting forces with Jesus having gone the other. If the disciples thought that their only options were to flee or to fight, the church is similarly beset by the constraints of this binary choice.[4] Its imagination is similarly limited when it thinks it either must rescue Jesus or leave him to fight his own battles. Both options are determined by the logic of force and violence. Both assume that there is nothing to be done that cannot be accomplished by violence. For those who fight, the fighting is the clear instrument of control of future events, the way of bending history in the right direction, the

4. For a helpful exposition of the Sermon on the Mount showing why these do not constitute the only options, see Walter Wink, *Engaging the Powers: Discernment and Resistance in a World of Domination* (Minneapolis: Fortress, 1992), 175–257.

answer to the crisis of the cross. Fighters want the glory of the kingdom without the Servant King. Likewise, those who flee have an equal belief in the determinative role of violence in history, only they abandon history to those who exercise it. Those who flee are often only those who would fight if they thought they could win. They may be more realists than cowards.[5] The one who heroically cut off the slave's ear surely fled too. History is given over to the power of violence even before the choice is made to flee or to fight, since both responses accord with the logic of violence.

Nevertheless, like the disciples in Gethsemane, the church is meant to be a church that prayerfully prepares for the moment of crisis that tests its resolve to follow Jesus, even to the cross. Rather than fleeing or fighting, the martyr-church is characterized by following. Jesus rouses sleeping disciples with the words "Rise, let us be going; see, my betrayer is at hand" (14:42). Jesus intended for his disciples to follow him at the moment of betrayal, to prepare for it in prayer throughout the night, to share in the cup of suffering as they had shared in the cup of fellowship. The church at prayer is the church in preparation for crisis, but it also learns that prayer is more than this. Christian prayer is itself an act of following insofar as the church learns to pray by imitating how Jesus prayed. As Jesus prayed in preparation for obedience to the Father, his very prayer was obedience. In the same way, Christians do not just act out the rituals of obedience ahead of time, but their obedience is already a ritual performance of imitating Christ. This

5. This is why Gandhi thought that only those who were willing to fight could truly be nonviolent. Otherwise, nonviolence becomes indistinguishable from cowardice. On the other hand, as Aristotle knew, the display of courage is never obvious, since one who is willing to fight may only be an injudicious fool.

means that imitating Jesus in the garden by praying is inseparable from imitating Jesus in suffering.

In Mark, though, refusing the binary choice of fighting or fleeing is symbolized only by two disciples who continue to follow, though in incomplete ways. The first is the young man who follows Jesus after everyone else forsakes him and flees; the second is Peter himself, who "followed him at a distance."

> And they all forsook him, and fled. And a young man followed him, with nothing but a linen cloth about his body; and they seized him, but he left the linen cloth and ran away naked. And they led Jesus to the high priest; and all the chief priests and the elders and the scribes were assembled. And Peter had followed him at a distance, right into the courtyard of the high priest; and he was sitting with the guards, and warming himself at the fire. (14:50–54)

The young man's following leads to his being seized in the same way that Jesus was, though he then flees at that moment. The others had fled at an earlier point, forsaking Jesus, not only displaying their lack of solidarity with the Jesus movement but also showing their belief that the movement was being destroyed. Both the arresting party and the disciples who flee take Jesus to be a violent insurrectionist. The former think that they need weapons to arrest Jesus, and the latter show that they are right. But the ones who rely on weapons, on both sides, fail to appreciate the kind of king that Jesus is. They locate him on the same political horizon as Rome and Rome's enemies, the temple and the temple's enemies. But an enemy of one regime is only too obviously a mirror image of that regime when its strategy of revolt, its tools for accomplishing it, and its "new"

89

political philosophy require predictable opposition, the kinds of rebellion for which it is already prepared.[6]

If the assumption that the authorities were interested in arresting only Jesus and not the disciples leads to the conclusion that the disciples were never meant to follow Jesus to the cross, it is an assumption that does not share the logic of the Jesus movement. Jesus predicts the fulfillment of the words "I will strike the shepherd, and the sheep will be scattered" (14:27; c.f. Zech. 13:7), but this simply describes the logic of how to quell a political rebellion that relies on traditional uses of power and violence. It reflects the understanding of instrumental following carried out by those who are on the winning side but only so long as it looks as though their side is winning. Seizing the leader means the end of the movement for those movements in which the sacrifice of the king is antithetical to the establishment of the next kingdom. The leader's loss of power marks a loss of hope for his followers insofar as it is taken for granted that his power is their hope, that his ability to evade arrest is their ability to persist as rebels, that his victory in battle is their share in the victorious new government.

The young man who begins to follow the arrested Jesus is immediately caught up in martyr imagery. The linen cloth that he wears and then quickly sheds reappears in the hands of Joseph of Arimathea for wrapping Jesus's dead body (15:46). For the young man, the cloth would have prefigured his sharing in Christ's death, having followed Jesus through the garden to the cross.

6. Max Weber showed how what Jacques Ellul called "anti-revolutionaries" positioned Marxism against capitalism using the identical theoretical forms of capitalism itself in a way that rendered inevitable the devolution into Soviet repression. See David Harvey's summary of Weber in *The Condition of Postmodernity: An Enquiry into the Origins of Cultural Change* (Oxford: Blackwell, 1990), 45.

It would have referred to his refusal to abandon Jesus to solitary suffering and his belief that the kingdom comes in the glory of obedience and sacrifice. But leaving the linen cloth at the site of seizure instead shows the young man's reluctance to be arrested, tried, and killed. There is no question that his arrest would have meant his death, and that is the reason he must shed the linen at this point. Treating the young man as a cameo appearance of Mark himself, as some scholars do, ignores the literary work that Mark achieves in the scene. It also misses the reappearance of the young man at the empty tomb, clothed this time in a martyr's white robe (16:5). This will be discussed in chapter 6. At this point, however, having successfully escaped, there is no possibility that the young man will be made to undergo martyrdom.

Moreover, the shed linen of a disciple is a disciple's shame. The would-be follower of Jesus runs away naked, stripped of the dignity otherwise provided by the fibers of solidarity with the death of Christ. When the church cannot imagine that it might die that death, it not only ceases to follow Christ but does so exposed and ashamed. It leaves the risk of being misunderstood and hated to Jesus himself and refuses to share in it. It hands Jesus over to suffering, believing that suffering was only for him. It is grateful for the sacrifice of the cross but even more grateful that someone else did it "for us" and "instead of us." It sleeps soundly in the garden, not understanding that it will be called on to resist fighting and fleeing, since fighting and fleeing are such natural responses that they require no prayer. Such a church fails to follow, sheds the linen, but justifies its having done so on grounds that there is nothing that following Jesus requires that he did not do on his own. This is a Christian life without cost, in which the stakes are low, the hazards disappear from view, and the demands are adjusted accordingly.

To its shame, the church readily discards its linen clothes but retains its body. In a different idiom, it turns one cheek but not the other; it forgives seven times but not eight; it gives a coat but not a cloak; it walks one mile but not two. It keeps a reserve of scarce goods and limited resources for a rainy day. The limit of its Christian life is reached too early when it exchanges one mode of protection for another: the dignity of a solitary linen garment for the freedom of the body. Here the scales of Christian discipleship measure according to a bounded economy that admits of a rigid margin for anxiety of what lies beyond, a frontier of fear. Some things are given up and others are retained in the name of self-preservation. The young man went further than the others did by being able to give up his clothes, but he could not endure giving up the only thing he was left with—his body.

In contrast, the martyr-church freely offers its body in the knowledge that its body is always already the broken body of Christ. It learns to resist the temptation to abandon Jesus by practicing faithfulness to the body. It rehearses the garden in the upper room. It eats its meals together, sharing in one bread, and so is constituted as one body. Its body is built up precisely to the extent that the bread is broken down, torn, and then digested. Like baptism, not only is the Eucharist a preparation for Christian death, but it is so by constituting a new kind of life, unbounded by fear.[7]

It is no accident that the Last Supper immediately precedes the temptations of the garden. The existence of

7. For two extraordinary accounts of how this is the case, see William T. Cavanaugh, *Torture and Eucharist: Theology, Politics, and the Body of Christ* (Oxford: Blackwell, 1998), and Samuel Wells, *God's Companions: Reimagining Christian Ethics* (Oxford: Blackwell, 2006).

the church takes its place as prior to that of its individual members, freeing them from the uncertainty and randomness of their individual deaths. The limitations that fearing death imposes are revealed to be nothing other than the posturing of rebellious powers for whom the extremities of control are shown not to extend beyond the anxieties of a people who do not have the Eucharist. By sharing in the body and blood of Christ, the church shares in its death *within* the life of the church. This means that the life of the church axiomatically precedes the life of the individual disciple, because even before it happens, the death of the disciple is taken up into the death of Christ.

This might seem again to suggest that martyrdom is rendered unnecessary or even impossible. After all, if disciples' deaths are taken up into the death of Christ, there would seem to be no reason for the disciple to die. It is true that there is no *reason* for disciples to die, in that they will not accomplish anything by their deaths. But this is not sufficient to keep them from becoming martyrs, since, as will be discussed later, martyrs do not die for "reasons." Moreover, we can learn something about salvation here. Salvation is not the result of the martyr's death, but not because Christians are saved from having to become martyrs. Rather, martyrdom is possible only for a people who have been saved through a death other than their own.[8] Christian martyrs do not try to become martyrs, as if there were anything at stake that could be caused or effected in their deaths. This would only perpetuate the most pervasive human delusion:

8. This can only be the case insofar as the Eucharist truly is a sacramental enactment, as Karl Rahner observes in *On the Theology of Death* (New York: Herder and Herder, 1961): "If the sacraments, in fact, perform the work which they symbolically express, then this sacrament [the Eucharist], in which we announce the mystery of his death, must effect his death in us" (76).

93

that we can save ourselves. It would only be to share in the pagan anxiety that the gods cannot grant eternal life. Instead, martyr-deaths are *merely* witnesses to the death of Christ in the same way that a living witness bears witness to Christ. Unlike those who watched the crucifixion of Christ from a safe distance, martyrs are not witnesses who only give verbal confirmation to the truth of the gospel, but they undergo the same fate involved in their gospel proclamation. That their testimony is "still alive" despite their deaths is a miracle Christians call resurrection.

As a result, the point is not that Christian deaths are rendered impossible by the death of Christ, somehow leaving behind only solitary fragments of extinguished individual existences. It is only to confirm that when Christians die the death of Christ, they do so having already committed their deaths to the ongoing story and life of the church. Eucharist signals the permission of those who share it to tell the stories of each others' lives and deaths as witnesses of the church. Individual deaths that share in the death of Christ are promised to remain within the testimony of the church rather than being lost to the void of dashed hopes for those who had wished for more from life.

Moreover, when it shares in the body of Christ, the church celebrates that the bread it breaks is not in short supply. It believes that the miracle of the loaves extends into the miracle of death and new life. Breaking and dividing does not mean waste and poverty; distribution does not mean depletion; consumption does not mean exhaustion. The loss of bread, like the loss of life, names a free expenditure in the face of the promise for restoration. The church gives away its bread as it gives away its body—in the hope of the resurrection by which its common life is renewed with replenished resources and in

94

which its suffering members are preserved in its witness to the world through the same miracle. "We break this bread to share in the body of Christ" is first a recognition of the frailty and vulnerability of its life together. It is not impervious to the power of the world to destroy its unity or wound its flesh. But with these words, the church also confesses its belief that broken bread does not lead to no-bread, that its martyred members are not silent members, that its frailty is met with the promise of resurrection. It does not exchange weakness for power or stop sharing bread in an attempt to shore up for itself the remnants of its remaining strength. Instead, it gives of itself all the more freely to the extent that its memory of the Father's faithfulness to the Son is enacted in the very constitution of its existence.

Individual bodies that feed on the body of Christ through incorporation and participation no longer belong to individual disciples; they belong to the church. This is a loss only insofar as the fear that death names continues to be a basis for making decisions about how to live. But the body's churchly incorporation makes plain that living according to the logic of death is no way to live. Ironically, the church is not permitted to shed its garment but retain its body, for it gains its life only by losing it. This is most ironic exactly at this point, because, as for the young man, trying to preserve the body inevitably means being cut off from the community of the most decisive body, though *this* body is perennially broken and put to death. The disciple's life is lost through participation in the broken bread of the cross, the fate of the martyr-church.

One of the reasons it is so easy to think that the cross was only for Jesus is that this is actually the way it happened in the Gospels. The disciples *do* abandon Jesus, only to be reunited with him after the resurrection. They

95

flee from the garden, but they seem to wait around. It is tempting to interpret the way things happened as an indication of the way it was supposed to happen. It is easy to think that the plan all along was for Jesus to undergo something terrible that only he was preparing for when he prayed in Gethsemane: that only he was meant to be arrested, that only he was to be beaten and carry a cross and bleed upon it. In this way, disciples are witnesses to the events because they watch them happen, not because they endure them alongside their master. They are not a community of followers but a mass of onlookers. In Mark, the only one who shares in the cross of Christ is Simon of Cyrene, who is compelled by the Romans to do so (15:21). But he represents only the failure of the disciples to take up their own crosses, since, like them, Simon is not made to die on one.

If the cross is not for disciples, we may also wonder what Jesus expected them to pray for in the garden. They were told to watch and pray to avoid temptation (14:38). Of course their temptation was to do the very thing that they ended up doing: failing to follow in arrest. They were not only positioned as Jesus's sentries, protecting him for the important work of speaking with the Father. Rather, they too were to pray to the Father that they would be able to share in the cup with the Son. The earlier question "Are you able to drink the cup that I drink?" (10:38) was only ostensibly answered in the affirmative. The temptation was to associate this cup with glory and so fail to pray against the temptation to drink the cup of suffering. It is only a version of this failure that says that the cup of suffering was only ever for Jesus anyway.

In the gospel idiom, martyrs die the death of Christ along with him. But as the story of desertion in the garden makes plain, no one actually does this. There is no faithful church at the cross. This is part of the suffering of the cross itself. Not only is the Son separated from the Father, but the church is not faithful to the Son of the Father; the abandonment is total. The church is a naked body, fleeced even of the cloth that would become a robe of righteousness. Furthermore, not only is the church deprived of access to God on account of the Son's separation from the Father, but also, to its shame, it cannot access the Father because it is not at the side of the Son. Leaving the Son is no way to get to the Father.

5

WATCHING FROM
A DISTANCE

I have stressed repeatedly that the cross is the height of glory. Rather than dashing hopes for the coming kingdom, the cross is already itself the kingdom come. If this is correct, then we have already seen the cross in the transfiguration of Jesus in front of three disciples. On the mountain, those three witnessed but did not understand that which they would later fail to witness due to their misunderstanding. Fleeing would mean their nonavailability with Jesus at the cross. Deserting would mean being deprived of the opportunity to complete the way that they were being included as witnesses of the glory of Christ. The disciples ceased to be his companions when he came in glory because they did not understand what a cross could have to do with glory. Just as they often followed Jesus at a distance on the road, so some of his followers watched the crucifixion from a distance. In both cases, they did not understand, and so they struggled to follow.

In Mark, misunderstanding is often symbolically related to blindness. The disciples' inability to understand the meaning of feeding the crowds—"Do you not yet understand?" (8:21)—is immediately followed by the healing of a blind man. Likewise, the misunderstanding shown in James's and John's request is contrasted with the sight of a blind man and, therefore, of his understanding and faith:

> "What do you want me to do for you?"
> "Grant us to sit, one at your right hand and one at your left, in your glory."
> "You do not know what you are asking." (10:36–38)
>
> "What do you want me to do for you?"
> "Master, let me receive my sight."
> "Go your way; your faith has made you well." And immediately he received his sight and followed him on the way. (10:51–52)[1]

These are two completely different understandings of what Jesus can and will "do for you." Blind Bartimaeus of Jericho had more understanding than the sons of Zebedee because he saw that Jesus's works of mercy are not ancillary to his mission but constitutive of it. This is demonstrated in Bartimaeus's faith and in Jesus's subsequently granting him his sight.

The same motif extends into requests for signs. The Pharisees were preoccupied with the requirement for a sign from Jesus in their attempt to discredit him (8:11).

---

1. Text from these two passages has been modified slightly to highlight the dialogue.

100

In the end, the only sign they are given is by Judas: "Now the betrayer had given them a *sign*, saying, 'The one I shall kiss is the man; seize him and lead him away under guard'" (14:44, emphasis added). In both cases, seeing is made to function in opposition to Jesus. The use of vision for discerning a sign about Jesus actually selects his enemies, functioning as a sign of their hostility. In the first case, Jesus refuses to give a sign to the Pharisees; they would not have believed anyway. They are not his followers because they are in search of something particular in Jesus, something decided ahead of time: a sign, a confession, an explanation. In each case, the seekers do not find what they want: a sign is not given, Jesus gets up and departs. Jesus's seekers are his enemies precisely because they seek him, and by seeking him, they attempt to control him.[2] In the case of Judas, the sign of friendship is turned into a sign of betrayal, since it is enlisted for a much more sinister purpose. These instances point to a common Markan theme, that the vision of disciples is not for controlling, that seeing Jesus is not for grasping at him. On the cross, Jesus is again asked for a sign by the chief priests and scribes.

> And with him they crucified two robbers, one on his right and one on his left. And those who passed by derided him, wagging their heads, and saying, "Aha! You who would destroy the temple and build it in three days, save yourself, and come down from the cross!" So also the chief priests mocked him to one another with the scribes, saying, "He saved others; he cannot save himself. Let the Christ, the King of Israel, come down now

2. Christopher Burdon shows that "seek" or "seeking" in Mark's Gospel is always an attempt to control (*Stumbling on God: Faith and Vision through Mark's Gospel* [Grand Rapids: Eerdmans, 1990], 47f). Other Gospels, of course, make more positive use of these words, such as in "seek and you shall find."

101

from the cross, that we may *see and believe*," (15:27–32, emphasis added).

In Mark's Gospel, it is precisely those who do not see and still believe—that is the "blind"—who receive their sight. But to those who ask to see rather than to understand, their request is not granted. Those who require a sign in order to believe will misunderstand the sign, and so it will not be given to them. Coming down off the cross would have constituted, for the chief priests and scribes, a kind of proof, but it would have only confirmed their prejudices since, like almost everyone else in the Gospel, they could not "see" the connection between the cross and glory.

All Christians have likewise had to reckon with the fact that the glory of the cross is difficult to see. The cross is the failure of Jesus's mission, a symbol of his inability to establish his kingdom, his impotence to follow through on his threats and promises. These were the thoughts of the original disciples as well as Jesus's executioners. But Christians also know that the resurrection comes next and so are quick to take Jesus down off the cross, betraying a fundamental unease with the presence of the cross. We quickly rush past Good Friday to Easter. This too is a symptom of our inability to see the cross as the height of Jesus's glory. It points to our reluctance to let Jesus be the servant who suffers nonviolently and prematurely directs our sights toward the kind of triumph that proves to the world that he was right after all. However, as we will see in the next chapter, Mark will not have any of this. The risen Christ is not "seen" at all in Mark's Gospel. If we have failed to see the glory on the cross, we will not be permitted to bend the resurrection to our conquering purposes.

Yet there is also a way of too glibly seeing the glory of the cross. Christians accustomed to the presence of crosses in worship may find themselves forgetting the terrible forsakenness and abandonment that the cross symbolizes. Being blessed with the sign of the cross may fail to bring to mind the paradox in which the cross was originally for one who was cursed (Deut. 21:22–23; Gal. 3:13). Not only was it obviously a punishment for crime, but it indicated abandonment by God. Jesus's rejection was thoroughgoing, as he said it would be (Mark 8:31). He did not just suffer; he was abandoned in his suffering. So Christians are tempted to close the gap between our experience and Jesus's cross with sorrow, by feeling sorry for Jesus, by thanking him for doing something that was exceedingly difficult. But this repeats the mistake I have observed earlier: it underwrites the assumption that Jesus's suffering was not meant to be shared by his disciples. Against this mistake, it is necessary to realize that the gap between Christian experience and the cross is closed by suffering *with* Jesus. The invitation to martyrdom comes to the church even, and especially, from the cross itself, not only in the life leading up to it or in the risen life beyond it.

In this way, the church is not entitled to make of the cross a symbol of victory in the absence of its own participation in it. But it would be an even greater mistake to imagine that its participation in Christ's suffering makes the cross a victory. The church's fellowship and solidarity with Christ are enacted in its suffering with him, but its actions do not add anything to Christ's suffering. This would only fetishize human pain and promote the church's self-indulgence. Following Jesus all the way to the cross, in other words, does not elevate an experience of happiness in the midst of suffering, nor does it suggest that suffering is really a good to be sought. Rather, Christian fellowship with Jesus is fellowship in his rejection. Solidarity in his death is still death. Jesus's loneliness is partly a function of the abandonment of his friends, but at the same time, it is not overcome by the fellow suffering and solidarity of his friends as martyrs. This simply means that the "answer" to human suffering is not more human suffering. Bearing one's cross is not a way to defeat crosses.

In this respect Christian crosses differ from the cross of Christ. Therefore, it would seem that in order to keep from exactly identifying the deaths of martyrs with the death of Jesus, we would need to explain why Jesus had to die. And must we not also be able to give some account of why Jesus died if we are to be permitted to attribute glory to it? After all, we feel as if we ought to understand what God was doing with the cross. There is a great urge to *explain* the cross, to speak about it as though it were a requirement, to claim that Jesus underwent it out of necessity. This urge corresponds to our desire to bring God's actions within the scope of our knowledge. It reflects our tendency to domesticate the wildness of God's acts by incorporating them in the purview of theory. We cannot stand to accept the cross of Christ as an empirical fact, as a historical event described by a bald and plain narrative unadorned with the trappings of religion.

But attempts of this kind are bound to fail. We come close but finally must refrain from saying that they *must* fail if the cross is to remain the cross. We come close to this because we rightly suspect that the cross must remain a contradiction, a sharp point of contrast within the world of human contestations for power, a reversal of accepted methods for accomplishing things. We know that the cross shows the impossibility of Christ finally to be overcome by the world precisely in the very moment of the world's apparent victory. We preserve the freedom of the Son in pure obedience to the Father and its exposure of all the world's slavery to disobedience. The dignity of the cross continues to animate Christian worship despite its horror, and when we acknowledge that this is so, we

104

are right to think that Christian worship has this quality of dignity despite horror by express virtue of the cross it celebrates. An explained cross "makes sense," our horror is mitigated, the scandal of Jesus's failure is allayed. To say that Jesus "came to die" says too much, even as a retrospective conclusion.

We are right to come close to saying that attempts to explain the cross *must* fail for these reasons. Nevertheless, we will finally have to refrain from affirming this. If explanations must fail, then this is because we have relied on another explanation that has succeeded. If we have discovered that it is impossible to derive a final meaning from the cross, then we have done so on the basis of another possibility: our confidence in the static nature in which some things are possible and others are not. We are thrust into a dialectical situation of affirming some things through their opposites while not quite being able to affirm the necessity of those opposites.

This can be seen to be the case regarding the cross in a number of respects. The cross is an act of violence, though violence is not necessary to the work of the cross. It is a point of weakness, but the power of the strong is irrelevant to it. Likewise, it is an act of God's grace, though God's gifts are not determined by those who would kill. Human sin was responsible for the cross, since Jesus would not have been crucified if we had not killed him sinfully. But Adam's sin did not *cause* Jesus to dwell among us.[3] This gives us too much credit and

3. This is, to be sure, a question with a long theological history. But see Robert W. Jenson, *Systematic Theology* (Oxford: Oxford University Press, 1997), 1:171–74. Jenson argues that the Son would have dwelt with creation even if Adam had not sinned since the question addresses not only redemption but also creation, two concepts that ought not to be treated without reference to each other. The incarnation crucially is part of the *fulfillment* of initial creation rather than its mere *restoration*, an idea that accords with Barth's insistence that creation and redemption are both derived from God's *single*

exalts our role as agents in our own salvation.[4] Affirming the dialectical way that Christians must proceed in thinking about the cross clarifies what it means to speak of the cross as a site of glory. Glory is something basked in, soaked up, rolled around in; it is a cause of fear, of joy, of wonder; but it resists being rendered explicable in light of something else.

The cross is disarmingly simple. Paul preached Christ crucified and not, we assume, a deeper insight to which the cross points, a more fundamental observation about human nature, a theology of the cross, a soteriology. We know that the cross was in some sense "for us," though we are not exactly sure how. Nevertheless, not being sure how the cross was for us does not change the fact that it was, nor does it preclude the participation of Christians as martyrs. Martyrs have not understood the purpose of the cross, closing the gap with their minds. They have understood, however, that following Jesus may involve hostility with the world and solidarity with Jesus in his death.

This is a reminder that theologians will not necessarily make the best martyrs. In fact, it is a warning that our theology may positively prevent Christian action. When it tries to do too much, it will obstruct the church's

---

and *undivided* decision. Von Balthasar comments that, for Barth, this is the foundation of his whole doctrine of creation. See Hans Urs von Balthasar, *The Theology of Karl Barth* (San Francisco: Ignatius, 1992), 204.

4. Making sin the starting point dies hard. Reinhold Niebuhr thought that doing so is a courageous move on account of its realism. But beyond anything else that might be said against making sin the starting point, doing so makes the "joy" of the cross (Heb. 12:2) inexplicable. Such joy as Jesus anticipated in the exaltation is not a reactive emotion that depends on suffering, and despite the fact that resurrection followed crucifixion for Jesus, its cosmic application indicates the surplus involved in what was much more than overcoming the cross through an exact reversal. The resurrection spills over from the space carved out by the cross, and its overflow makes the gospel good news.

obedience in response to the demand for faithfulness that meets the church in one free and spontaneous moment. Like the best preaching, good theology will enable the church to be faithful; it will ignore those questions that are purely academic and speculative. It will not presume that just because it can respond to a question, its doing so will exhaust the fullness of any answer. It will humbly admit the limits of its own exercise and excuse itself from discussion when it comes between the call of God and the response of the church.[5]

The limits of theology are best seen in the cross. As the indisputable crux of Christian belief, indeed of the whole world, the cross has possibly elicited more dangerous speculation and perilous, empty words than any other subject in the Christian confession. It is as though the closer into its orbit theologians fly, the more their otherwise reliable instruments freeze up and fail them. The cross exposes our penchant for idolatry in the guise of theology, our pretentious clamoring after reassurance, our crude tactics for figuring things out by tearing them apart to see what makes them tick only to be left with empty centers and evacuated wholes. Our methods will often yield free-floating words, detached from their uses in church practice, in prayer, in liturgy. They will be put to use for constructing impressive edifices and towering theoretical structures, but these will only crumble for being hollow.

It is important to have before us the incomprehensible cross in order to make room for the declaration that it is characterized by glory. Our inability to fix the meaning of the cross is, in some ways, the very meaning of the

5. In saying that theologians will not necessarily make the best martyrs, I am obviously not trying to let theologians off the hook, since we will surely also have to conclude that theologians who cannot become martyrs have also failed as theologians.

cross. But it is not a meaning that bends to our logic or our understandings of how transactions work, of how the Son relates to the Father, or of how human sin forces the hand of God. Rather, the inexplicability of the cross radically intensifies the call to carry crosses and follow Jesus in suffering, since it does not rely on a belief in the intrinsic reasonableness of suffering.

If the cross made sense, we would be tempted to bear our own crosses for the wrong reasons, and in practice we would put those reasons to use in refusing to bear them. The church deceives itself into thinking that only Jesus had to suffer the cross when it has produced atonement theories that explain what the cross of Christ means, that his special vocation required a unique sacrifice, that his mission of redemption necessitated a payment to Satan that only he could pay, or that only he could appease the wrath of God on behalf of humanity. Theology of this sort no doubt serves a purpose and should not be avoided in principle. Moreover, there are certainly attempts within the New Testament itself to make sense of the cross, to clarify what it did, how it was a sacrifice, what it means for us, and how it relates to the resurrection. But it is equally instructive to ponder why Mark, for instance, does not do this. His Gospel comes closest in the words of Jesus concerning his death as a "ransom for many" (10:45). But readers are left to speculate what this could mean, sometimes to their own confusion.

Mark not only refuses to accommodate our proclivity to tame Jesus's suffering through explanation. His Gospel also refuses to explain suffering as such.[6] We

6. Rowan Williams points to how explanations of the suffering of the cross can easily be construed as legitimating the rightness of the sufferer. See Williams, *Resurrection: Interpreting the Easter Gospel* (London: Darton, Longman and Todd, 2002), 70.

have difficulty naming what it is that makes Jesus's death redemptive, what makes it good news for us, but this is not because we possess a more general notion that attributes meaning to it all. We are not given an insight that underscores something intrinsically good about suffering. Instead, the call for the church to follow Jesus in the cross, to suffer with him, does not derive from theory but from the conviction that our efforts are not finally determinative of outcomes, that God is good, and that the victory of his kingdom is not brought about in the usual manner. The question of the cross's meaning is a question that can be answered only in practice.

Like the original disciples, all Christians are asked to suffer for and with Jesus because of their friendship with him. One remarkable characteristic of friendship is that it cannot be reduced to explanations. We call explainable friendships relationships of convenience, showing that they are not truly friendships at all but only contractual agreements marked by predictable and reciprocal transactions. When one party fails to uphold his side of the contract, the contract is broken and the other party is released from its obligation. Forgiveness and love are not constitutive elements. But this is not the case with friendships. Friends do not love each other for some more basic or original purpose; they do not share a status that is easily nullified. Jesus's cross may have been a failure of his mission in which his friends shared, but he did not betray his friends in his failure. His friendship *was* his mission. This helps us understand the tragedies of Judas's betrayal and Peter's denial. They forsook Jesus's friendship and therefore his cross.

All of this means that our friendship with God is more basic to God's way in the world than any actions describable in transactional terms. Once we have

109

rationalized our friendship with God, we have freed ourselves from continuing to abide in it. Once we have explained why we are his friends, we have actually explained why we do not need his friendship. Like Job, who was tested to see whether he feared God "for naught" (Job 1:9) and so underwent suffering that defied the rationalizations of his so-called friends, Christians are those whose love for Jesus is demonstrated by carrying crosses for naught, for no reason at all save for their love of Jesus.

In this, the church is reminded that its refusal to use violence against its enemies when it is persecuted is not a function of an overriding belief in the power of nonviolence but is a way of loving Jesus. As with the actions of any lover for the loved one, the church performs its acts of love to God irrespective of any intrinsic qualities of those acts. Lovers' acts are expressions of love and can properly be understood only as such. We are opened up to the possibility of suffering, of being wounded, through friendship and love. Christ's persistence in calling us his friends and in not overwhelming us with the force reserved for use against one's enemies is what is meant by the claim that he offered his life for sinners and underwrites Paul's reflections on the cross.

> While we were still weak, at the right time Christ died for the ungodly. Why, one will hardly die for a righteous man—though perhaps for a good man one will dare even to die. But God shows his love for us in that while we were yet sinners Christ died for us. (Rom. 5:6–8)

Christ's appeal of friendship was not extinguished by our refusal. That we would refuse the appeal may have been inevitable, since we do not know how to be friends with enemies. But our refusal cannot be rendered logically necessary to our friendship with God. God's offer was love; our response was violence. Any attempts to explain the cross will therefore become attempts to explain God's love. That alone is quite impossible, of course, but it is further made ridiculous by the fact that God's love is not separable from God's very selfhood and existence, meaning that in order to explain the cross we would have to explain God!

We may now summarize how glory, friendship, and nonviolent suffering are related for Christians. All defy explanation and resist being described in instrumental terms. Instead, they are described only as expressions of love. Glory is the effect of the reciprocal love of the Father for the Son; friendship is how the church is related to Jesus and shares in his glory; nonviolent suffering is the shape of that friendship and the cost of glory.

Overcoming blindness and misunderstanding is a correlative condition of our friendship with Jesus, our refusal to seize him with our vision. The ability to see the cross as glorious is a skill that the church takes upon itself as a function of its way of life and the training of subsequent generations of Christians. Having eyes to see the kingdom come at the cross results from cultivating the vision necessary to follow Jesus on the road to it. In this way, we might speak about an aesthetics of the cross according to which the church recognizes glory without either relying on cosmic explanations or objectifying suffering. The cross is neither rational nor objectively beautiful. Paul knew that attempts to make it these things are attempts to mitigate the cross's effect as a scandal, a stumbling block to those who would otherwise believe (1 Cor. 1:23). But the problem is that they would believe the wrong thing. Or, worse, they

111

would be allowed to believe without engaging in the practices of worship, prayer, and self-denial necessary to be able to stumble on the cross and yet not fall.

Perhaps the most determinative church practice for encountering the cross is found in its preaching. When the word of God is preached, it is made present to listeners who are confronted with a moment of decisive choice: whether they have ears to hear the word as an invitation or a piece of entertainment, a word to themselves or a good story about others, whether it elicits involvement or apathy. When the cross is preached, the listener is preeminently struck and immobilized, stumbles and falls, or else clamors after deeper, reductive meanings.[7]

But the moment of choice is a moment in a particular history. Hearers of the cross preached are not isolated from the church's timeful existence. There is nothing particularly sacred about the moment in which the word is preached and heard, even though this may be the moment of conversion and repentance. Instead, the church locates its preaching of the cross within the much larger narrative of Jesus's life and ministry, an account of its own existence as the church, its routine practices of worship and fellowship, and its regard for scripture. This allows Christians to preach the simplicity of the cross. The problem in this regard is often less that the cross is made to perform too small of a role in Christian existence and more that it becomes too determinative. This comment is not first about the importance of the cross but about its isolation from the life of Jesus. If Jesus's body and blood are shared

7. In Herbert McCabe's words, "The preaching of the gospel does not explain God to you. It makes you ready, open, vulnerable" (McCabe, *God, Christ, and Us* [New York: Continuum, 2003], 144).

but the story is not told of the woman washing his feet, the gospel is incomplete. Where some are baptized but their feet are not washed, the nature of Christ's servanthood will be distorted. Where Christians feed themselves but not others, the gospel will not be good news to the poor. Where the peace is passed but wounds are not bound up, forgiveness will be reserved only for one's friends. Not only can this fund a confusion that leads to the improbability of the church's martyr-witness, but it deprives the world of good news. These are ultimately bound up with each other.

The cross is simple for a church that has learned to tell stories rather than relay information. Martyrs are not killed for the information they speak but for the stories they narrate and claim to be true.[8] Like the lives and deaths of martyrs themselves, Jesus's death is part of a story that includes Abraham, Isaac, Jacob, Rahab, and Mary. There are prophets being fed in the wilderness, there are calls to leave one place and go to another, there is slavery and liberation of a particular people. Jesus can be accounted for genealogically. But this narrative cannot be boiled down to a few, or even many, key points. The narrative is not just about how God is transforming and has transformed the world; the narrative is itself part of how God transforms.[9] The

8. Writing in a different context, though making a parallel point, Augustine objected to those who elevated the mind as the sole determiner of what constitutes true knowledge. See *De Trinitate* 14.13.

9. See Julian Hartt, *Theological Method and Imagination* (New York: Seabury, 1977), 239. Likewise, Hans Frei states that this is a characteristic of meaning in the narrative genre: "Especially in narrative . . . where meaning is most nearly inseparable from the words—from the descriptive shape of the story as a pattern of enactment, there is neither need for nor use in looking for meaning in a more profound stratum underneath the structure (a separable 'subject matter')." Frei, *The Eclipse of Biblical Narrative: A Study in Eighteenth- and Nineteenth-Century Hermeneutics* (New Haven, CT: Yale University Press, 1974), 281. Nevertheless, it may be that narrative theology

113

impartation of new life does not correspond to the dissemination of knowledge, even in the sense that is commonly assumed by revelation. The new life in Christ is not a possession except insofar as a narrative can be possessed. Claiming that a narrative is "mine" differs from claiming to own information. I share information with you so that you can have it too, but your possession of my information does not include your life with mine. But the story of how God is transforming the world, the story in which the cross is located, is told by those who tell it as their own story. And their telling of it invites others to make it theirs too. The new life, therefore, is not enlightenment but transformation. It is not the product of internal ascension to a spiritual idea but results from daily encountering God in the world and choosing to follow and obey.

Like the cross itself, the cross preached is vulnerable. It is not obviously meaningful, compellingly true, strikingly beautiful, intuitively proper, nor observably rational. When it suffers defeat, that is to be expected. But if it is to be authentic preaching, its suffering of defeat will be crosslike. It will not self-righteously assert the irrationality of its message in order to condemn human reason, nor will it cease to offer its message in the face of rejection. But preaching the gospel is not persistent in order to get its way in the belief that the world will eventually give in. Rather, its persistence is a function of its hope in God, whose persistence was displayed on the cross and by the cross itself. The church is tempted to rebuff its crosses when it is tempted to curtail its preaching out of frustration, insularity, or insecurity. But it also does so when it is

---

has now run its course to the extent that it has tried to make too much of a genre apart from the particular narrative of Israel and Jesus.

tempted to secure its witness against vulnerability, to ensure its own survival for preaching the gospel by preaching an impervious message, an opaque dogma, and an imperial set of concerns.

This leads to the striking conclusion that the church can speak about the cross as having any meaning at all only if it is a martyr-church. Unless its life is characterized by the training and memory of those whose discipleship involves disharmony with the world's unbelief, whose way of life makes hostility understandable rather than unfathomable, then the cross of Christ has no meaning for the church. Notice, though, that this is not the same as claiming that the church's faithfulness *gives* the cross meaning or *makes* it true. This makes the cross the work of the church, refusing to follow or to allow Jesus to go ahead. Furthermore, as was observed above, it differs from saying that the church is entitled to the meaning of the cross by virtue of its theories. That would make the cross less than a scandal.

The church's witness to the cross cannot issue from any community other than those that embody the life of the cross. Otherwise its preaching would not be commendably simple, effortlessly reflecting the simplicity of the cross. Rather, it would be regrettably empty and meaningless. The cross's meaning is shown by those who live as though reality is disclosed by the self-denial of the Son of God. It is demonstrated by a people who take the time to recognize how the cross is the site of the Son's glorification. It is attested in the proclamation of those who sing about the kingdom come even though it is difficult to see, and our not seeing is a function of our not singing, of being found outside the way of life that made seeing possible. However, this conclusion cannot finally be argued; it can only be shown, seen, and demonstrated. If it could be argued, there would

115

be no need for witnesses. If the church could hold the meaning of the cross with words, it would not need to bear crosses. It would merely preach—but its preaching would not be true. It would have asked for a sign and have been found preaching the sign in falsehood rather than the gospel of one whose refusal to come down off the cross *is* a sign after all. But only for those with eyes to see it: just look at its terrible glory.[10]

10. See Ludwig Wittgenstein's example of why, after trying to convince someone else that a blossoming flower is marvelous, all you are left with is the appeal: "Just look at it opening out!" Wittgenstein, *Culture and Value*, trans. Peter Winch (Chicago: University of Chicago Press, 1984), 56e. Seeing glory no doubt admits to a carefully trained aesthetic that continues to look with love and wonder at things like flowers. This means that it is important to use the cross in worship, if only to learn how to look at it.

6

Πoτ Seeing
τhe Risen Oπe

The empty tomb in Mark is stark and disquieting. There is hardly joy and celebration; instead there is trembling and fear. In this, the message to the churches differs from that of the other Gospels in some respects. Mark's Gospel does not include any resurrection appearances; there is no reunion with the frightened disciples who had betrayed Jesus; there is no greeting of peace; there is no invitation to eat a breakfast of bread and fish around a charcoal fire on the shore of the lake.

Just as the church's own witness does not involve offering proofs, Mark does not confirm the reality of the resurrection by allowing readers to "see" Christ raised. The resurrected one does not speak, show his hands, or tell his followers what to do. The narrative does not appease the curiosity of readers but only asks them, together with the women at the tomb, to believe the testimony of the young man dressed in white. The book closes with the women's having only seen the empty tomb, but being promised to see the risen Jesus if they follow him to Galilee.

> And entering the tomb, they saw a young man sitting on the right side, dressed in a white robe; and they were amazed. And he said to them, "Do not be amazed; you seek Jesus of Nazareth, who was crucified. He has risen, he is not here; see the place where they laid him. But go, tell his disciples and Peter that he is going before you to Galilee; there you will see him, as he told you." And they went out and fled from the tomb; for trembling and astonishment had come upon them; and they said nothing to any one, for they were afraid. (16:5–8)

Here the mysterious figure is a "young man," not an angel as in other Gospels. The young man reappears from chapter 14, where he fled from being arrested in the garden. Earlier he had left his linen cloth behind in order to escape arrest, fleeing in shameful nakedness. Both the linen cloth and the young man were to appear later in the story, though not together.[1] As we have already seen, the linen cloth is used by Joseph of Arimathea for

---

1. Ched Myers, *Binding the Strong Man: A Political Reading of Mark's Story of Jesus* (Maryknoll, NY: Orbis, 1988), 368–69. On the literary level, Mark has constructed what Myers calls "regathering," the reemergence of disparate plot elements that cast meaning back over their earlier appearances in the plot. As Samuel Wells argues, this is the eschatological work of God, including the lost in God's story in such a way that their earlier confusion is narrated by the ending. See Wells's discussion of "reincorporation" in *Improvisation: The Drama of Christian Ethics* (Grand Rapids: Brazos, 2004). As I argue in this chapter, the ending of Mark's story is not the ending of the gospel, meaning that such elements will only finally be regathered outside of Mark's narrative. I take this to be what Myers means by speaking about a "hint" of regathering (368).

wrapping Jesus's dead body (15:46). It is the garment of the crucified, the appropriate clothing for a corpse. It was refused by the young man when he fled the garden. As a symbol of the church deserting Jesus at arrest, he also represents the church's refusal to stand in solidarity with Jesus in his suffering and death. Nevertheless, the young man reappears dressed in white, the color of martyrs, the color of Christ at the transfiguration, at the height of the glory of the cross.

Moreover, the young man is seated "on the right side." James and John had earlier argued over this position (10:37), and in his trial, Jesus spoke of the Son of Man's being seated on the right side of power (14:62). It is a clear reference to a position of supremacy and authority. But what James and John did not understand was that the action that entitled Jesus himself to that position—the cross—would be required of whomever else would share in that power. The young man thus symbolizes those who have endured the cross of Christ and now sit "on the right side" as a result. As for Jesus himself, the route to glory for disciples is not around death but through it, causing Christ to be "seated at the right hand of the Father," as the creeds put it. This is the position of the cosmic viceroy, a position of sovereignty over those who would claim to rule over human affairs and history.[2] It is in direct contrast to the political authority of Rome and the other nations, which persist in exercising power in the world only through posturing and usurping the claim of those who now reign with Christ. Those who now reign do so precisely on account of their having endured the

2. See John Howard Yoder, "How H. Richard Niebuhr Reasoned: A Critique of *Christ and Culture*," in Glen H. Stassen, Diane M. Yeager, and John Howard Yoder, *Authentic Transformation: A New Vision of Christ and Culture* (Nashville: Abingdon, 1996), 88.

suffering inflicted by those who only pretend to reign yet inflict suffering as a result.

Reclothed as a martyr, the young man bears witness to the resurrection as only the church can. Astonishingly, perhaps, he does not reveal the resurrected man in any plain way. He does not produce a body triumphant in beauty or radiant in glory. Instead, he reissues the call to discipleship, this time not to Jerusalem but back to Galilee. The story loops back to the beginning, where Jesus first called fishermen on the beach to "follow me" (1:17). As before, there is no alluring appearance to entice followers. Mark's resurrected Jesus would seem to match the Jesus who preached itinerantly in the hills of Palestine. For those at the concluding episode, the only thing to "see" with plain sight is the empty tomb: "See the place where they laid him." Of course, an empty tomb is not proof of the resurrection but only a place to begin from, a sign that points in another direction, a signal to look somewhere else. To truly "see" the resurrection requires discipleship, following behind Jesus as he goes ahead, refusing to be held even by the grasping vision of would-be witnesses.

It is important to see that the church is doubly represented in the final scene of Mark's Gospel. The young man is the martyr-church, a witness to the resurrection who does not offer proof but only directs attention to the continual forward progress of the resurrected one. He holds nothing, seemingly alone, absent the untamed Messiah whose movements are spoken of without being explained, narrated without being described. "He is going before you to Galilee" is way of indicating without curbing anticipation; there is a future promise to be fulfilled even, and especially, by one whose new life is unbounded by the world. The young man is a witness to an uncontrolled mystery. But the church is also represented by

120

the women who flee, as the young man did earlier in the story. In them the church is seen refusing to follow behind the resurrected Christ, fearing what it would mean, preserving their safety against the wildness of a man once dead and now living, securing their lives against the consequences of its witness.

The double representation shows the church as martyrs and also as those who refuse martyrdom. It suggests a contrast between those who see and those who do not. The latter, the women, fail to see because they fail to follow. As a result, they "said nothing to anyone." Their silence is a paradox: the martyr-church speaks despite the silencing of death, while the church refusing martyrdom has nothing to say though it keeps on living. But of course, this is just the paradox of resurrection. As the body of Christ, the church is implicated in the reversal undergone by Jesus himself. Despite having fled in the garden, the church inhabits the promise of being reunited with Jesus on the other side of death, even though it is still called to follow. The church is not absolved of its scattering, having secured its life by fleeing; instead it is given another chance to lose its life. The end of Mark's Gospel is the beginning again.

Furthermore, when the church speaks, it can speak only as the young man. It knows about the resurrection only on the basis of its life lived as church, which is to say that its faith is inherited from those who have come before in the church. In the same way, though ironically, since Mark is part of the church's scriptures, its knowledge of the resurrection owes to the witness of the church. There is no way to get behind the testimony of witnesses to the surer account of the event itself. Mark will not even show us the event: it is known only by the witness of the young man, the martyr-church. This means that the church must listen to itself. It trusts itself to the testimony of its own members; it listens to the stories of those who have gone before. When it reads the Christian scriptures, it is aware that it is reading a collection of witnesses produced by the church for the sake of the church's witness to the world. It does not read them looking only for answers to questions; it does not merely seek explanations. Instead, it subjects itself to the authority of the scriptures read as a product of the church's previous generations. It sees itself as part of a much larger story that enables today's readers to be vulnerable to the historic witness, not primarily of those who wrote the scriptural texts but of those who called those texts scripture.

Nevertheless, the church does not merely and uncritically adopt the testimony of its members. It does not simply take their word for granted on matters of testimony. This is because the witness of the church to each subsequent generation comes in the form not of proposition but of invitation. Propositions only name a variant of the tendency to ask questions and look for answers. Instead, the church trains its faculties to hear the questions of its members as invitations to see the risen Christ for itself. The resurrection life of the church is a life made possible by the resurrection. Seeing Jesus in Galilee is the invitation the church extends within its body, from those who have already seen to those who have not yet done so. The church listens to the young man's testimony, responds to his invitation to look for Jesus, who has gone ahead. In this way, Mark dramatically captures the tension of the church's own inner life, how it believes itself: not by earlier generations' passing down proof to later generations but by its bidding each generation to follow into places where it has been, though it may have only white robes as "proof."

The Gospel thus ends with uncertainty, unresolved. Many scholars have noted how it ends with a strange grammatical construction, a preposition, the kind of word that anticipates something to come after it. Others have produced apocryphal longer endings to resolve this problem. By doing so, they have wanted to give the Gospel both a grammatical and a narrative resolution.[3] They depict the women telling the male disciples; they show the risen Jesus speaking and giving instructions; they display the disciples being faithful. This reflects our temptation to have a complete story in which our role is purely optional. But Mark's Gospel will not be concluded with a page of written text since, after all, the whole book is merely "the beginning of the gospel" (1:1). The end is approached only through invitation and is realized only in practice.

The church cannot tell the gospel Mark tells without locating itself within Mark's narrative course of events. In this way, the young man is an eschatological sign, a reading back into the story of the reality of promise. The church is promised that its faithful witness is integral to the internal coherence of the Gospel's ability to function as a witness to others. In this way, its witness is a part of the very scripture that it reads as a witness to Christ. In faithfulness to the cause of Christ, the church's life and death are already given meaning *within the text*.

However, we can say this without granting to Mark's story a narrative closure. If the martyr-church is folded back into the narrative, it does not serve to make the story less ambiguous: it merely transforms the ambiguity from one to be solved by exegetes into one to be worked

3. On this theme, see the collection of essays in Beverly Roberts Gaventa and Patrick D. Milled, eds., *The Ending of Mark and the Ends of God: Essays in Memory of Donald Harrisville Juel* (Louisville, KY: Westminster John Knox, 2005).

out by witness. There is no assurance that the church will be marked by following rather than fleeing, since even our memory of the young man is still haunted by his abrupt flight. Whether the church plays the role of the women at the tomb or of the young man cannot be answered at the level of biblical interpretation, for that very question is left hanging as an open invitation, as if it were an incomplete sentence, a pause waiting for the next word to be spoken. Who will speak the next word? Or will there instead be silence, no word, no witness? The church is not assured of the answer, but it is promised the faithfulness of God if, in answering, it gets killed as a result.

The resurrection of Christ cannot be known in the world or in the church without the community of believers who resolve among themselves to bear witness to the resurrection. There is an appropriate circularity to this logic, which I have partially explored in earlier chapters. Among other things, there is a real sense in which the church testifies to itself. But this does not collapse the church into Christ completely. The resurrected church is not identical with the resurrected Christ. For one thing, the connection between the church and *its* resurrection is not the same as the connection between Christ and *his* resurrection. Paradigmatically represented by those who fled in the garden, the church is not in a position to accord itself a position alongside Jesus on other crosses. It is nothing more than speculation to ask whether the disciples, had they been faithful, would also have been raised with Jesus. Instead, the church is included in the resurrection of Christ through its share in his suffering and its share in the promise of being raised with him. This helps us understand the presence of the young man at the tomb dressed in martyr's clothes. We are not told whether he too has been raised, but it is at least clear that he would not be robed in white if not for his martyr-death, and he would not have borne witness if not for his inclusion in the promise of life that is made to martyrs.

All of this means that the church does more than bear witness to itself even though its ability to speak of Christ as raised is a function of its having followed Christ in suffering. Jesus remains "other" to the church, a stranger who goes ahead, who bids us follow, but who will not be constrained by our descriptions or by our best efforts to enlist him in our cause. The otherness of Jesus is not just preserved by the ambiguity of resurrection. The New Testament does not try to clarify for us what a "resurrection" means, just as it leaves "transfiguration" obscure. It does not enumerate the characteristics of a resurrected body. Jesus is not kept at a distance by this mystery; the mystery serves, in fact, to draw us into it. In the process, the secrets of mystery are not so much revealed as answers to obscure questions as they are constantly renewed for those who follow Jesus and who, in following, grow to understand how their lives as followers are possible only because the Son of Man has been raised.

The church is offered understanding without explanation. This is one of the crucial themes in Mark's Gospel. The enemies of Jesus know who he is and are against him: a demon declares, "I know who you are" (1:24), Pilate readily calls Jesus "King of the Jews" (15:9), the centurion makes a "confession" that Jesus is the Son of God on a cross (15:39). In contrast, his followers stammer their confessions and often speak nonsense out of fear. Nevertheless, they continually strive to understand and trust Jesus. Those in power grasp at Jesus without fear, opposing him, while those closest to him cautiously keep their distance, struggling to make sense of the mystery that goes before them.

The church can never claim to know definitively what a resurrection is—for example, how a risen Christ differs from a risen Lazarus. This is only because its participation and inclusion in the resurrection of Christ is an ongoing aspect of its life and mission.[4] The church participates in the risen life of Christ when it shares resurrection fellowship in breaking bread. A possible scenario for the continuing mission of the post-Easter church is captured in Luke's Gospel in the story of the disciples on the way to Emmaus (Luke 24). The disciples had heard about the empty tomb through the witness of the women but did not believe them, thinking they had told "an idle tale." Meeting Jesus on the road but not recognizing him, they "constrained him, saying, 'Stay with us,'" even though "he appeared to be going further" (24:28–29).[5] Over a meal, their eyes are opened when Jesus breaks the bread and vanishes from their sight. Their eyes see, but they are left holding only bread. This indicates that Jesus exists to the church as both a presence and an absence. The Eucharist is a mystery for this reason: it embodies the cross and resurrection of Christ within the church, including the church in the very body of Christ as shattered and exalted, but not in a way that allows the church to possess the meaning of its acts when it follows Christ in them.[6]

4. See Robert W. Jenson, *Systematic Theology*, vol. 1, *The Triune God* (Oxford: Oxford University Press, 1997), 200–201.

5. Luke Timothy Johnson dismisses the reference to Jesus's determination to go further, seeing it as a rhetorical element merely to enhance the storytelling. See *The Gospel of Luke* (Collegeville, MN: Liturgical, 1991), 396.

6. Hans Urs von Balthasar rightly discusses the Emmaus story within the phase of resurrection encounter with the disciples that is, in a sense, presacramental (since the forty days after the resurrection are relatively unmediated), while also inaugurating the sacramental time that was to follow. *A Theology of History* (San Francisco: Ignatius, 1994), 83–100.

Like the Emmaus disciples, the church is constantly tempted to make Jesus "stay with us," to possess him and control his movements. He vanishes because he had intended to go further, as for the women at the empty tomb in Mark. He was going ahead into Galilee, and "there you will see him." He will not be seen by a sight that grasps, but only by a vision that crosses the space between the disciple and Jesus with the movement of following. The church faces this temptation when it attempts to prove to the world that the resurrection has happened, when it builds a case for it on apologetic grounds, when it construes a logical defense for its belief. The problem is not only that such efforts may fail to convince anybody. Indeed, the attempt to win the argument on logical or juridical grounds is *meant to fail*, a point exemplified by the fact that women are entrusted to bear witness. The reliability of their testimony is disabled by their gender in that patriarchal milieu. And yet it is the women who are promised to see Jesus in Galilee, who had not abandoned Jesus at the cross, and who, Mark explains, had followed and served Jesus in Galilee (15:40–41). These unlikely witnesses are undermined in their authority for the same reason that Peter will later amaze the crowds at Pentecost: the proclamation of the gospel does not rely on the gender or education of the witnesses. After all, a gospel proclaimed by women and uneducated fishermen is a social sign of the cosmic reversal that the gospel heralds.[7]

If the church does not possess Jesus through its apologetics, it also acknowledges that its share in the resurrection is not a possession. We have already noted the disjunction between the resurrection of Christ and the resurrection of the church. The former is accounted to

7. Augustine, *City of God* 22.5.

127

the church's proclamation as its confession; that is, it is the news given to it to proclaim to the world. The church persists in proclaiming it even though it cannot claim with certainty to know what it means for somebody to be resurrected.[8] God has given his people such knowledge on the basis of faith, extended by invitation through witness. But the resurrection of the church is held on to by hope. It is the content of a believed promise that renounces claims to assert control over future events; there is no room for Christians to secure their own future except insofar as they relate their own resurrection hope to the confession of the empty tomb. There is no promise of Christian victory apart from being given a reign with Christ himself. This means that the power of the resurrection abjures all idolatry, since it is not constructed from assurances about the fate of the world. It is given only to Jesus, who goes ahead into Galilee, to reveal himself to those who have followed him there.[9]

This helps us to see that the logical distance between the two resurrections—the church's and Christ's—is traversed only by forgiveness. The Christian need for forgiveness is signaled by the inclusion of Peter in the Easter message: "Go, tell his disciples and Peter" (16:7). Just as the witness of the once-fugitive young man at the tomb embraces the lost community of shattered faith and failed commitments, so also Peter the denier is singled

8. See Rowan Williams, *Resurrection: Interpreting the Easter Gospel* (London: Darton, Longman and Todd, 2002), chap. 5.

9. In *Fools, Martyrs, Traitors: The Story of Martyrdom in the Western World* (New York: Alfred A. Knopf, 1997), Lacey Baldwin Smith profoundly misunderstands the connection between cross and resurrection because he forgets that the resurrection is known and told by those whose witness to it is bound up with their following in this way. For him, the cross and resurrection "establish martyrdom as a deliberate means to an end, and they prove it works" (72). In this book, I hope I have been saying much to counter this repugnant conclusion.

out for receiving the good news. He is not left weeping in the high priest's courtyard, nor is he passed over in favor of a more worthy disciple. The full inclusion of those who were scattered rewrites the logic of Christian identity in light of the resurrection. To be included in the resurrection life of Christ is to be forgiven for abandoning Jesus at the cross, and it is also to be given another chance to be faithful.

We should acknowledge that this appears to be a tension; it resembles the way in which the church is represented by both the women and the young man. On the one hand, the church is reapproached by God's grace in forgiveness despite prior abandonment. On the other hand, however, it is displayed as a church of martyrs. How can the church be characterized by both martyrdom and failure to suffer? Nevertheless, this is a tension only insofar as it is assumed that martyrs are heroes, that their ability to stand firm marks their own strength. The gift of forgiveness to the deserted church is identical with the gift to martyrs for declaring the gospel. In this way, the gospel is nothing but sheer grace, especially evident in those who know that they cannot endure on the basis of their own power. Put differently, the very ability to suffer martyrdom is itself a witness to the inclusion of the forsaken in the life of the resurrection.

The martyr-church is always a church that acknowledges its frailty, its inability to follow Jesus to the cross, and its receipt of forgiveness for failing to do so. It is frail because it would rather exchange the demands of the gospel for consolation from the world; its strength is depleted when it sleeps in the garden for lack of prayer. Likewise, it is absent from the cross because it fails to recognize God's generosity; its courage is sapped by its failure to understand. But, as forgiven, it accepts its failure and absence as part of the story it tells about its redemption. In doing so, the church acknowledges that its hope in resurrection is not an achievement. It has not earned the object of its hope, otherwise the object would not need to be hoped for. Instead, its life is thrust back upon the resurrected one in patient expectation that its future will be included in that resurrection. The two resurrections are thus held together without being confused; they are contingently related by trust, failure, and forgiveness.

If Jesus goes ahead, then the Christian life is not static. It is constantly on the move, not having arrived. When it has stopped moving, it is not because it has reached its destination but because it has clutched at idols. It has contented itself with dumb objects that do not speak and lame objects that have no motion. Striving to possess the God who goes ahead of the church into the unknown with only the simple words "Follow me," the settled Christian conviction is left to grasp inert things, motionless objects suitable for controlling but not for saving. "Saved" does not describe a state so much as a condition of a life of motion. The church seeks to live its life together both as already raised people and as those who realize that they have been raised only when they live the resurrection life.

But we want a sign. We want assurance that the Christian life has some payoff, that it is all true. As we saw in the last chapter, we are like the Pharisees. We would rather test Jesus than engage in a genuine and meaningful exercise (8:11). We want to side with Jesus in a practice match rather than stand with him in the main event. But Jesus counters the Pharisees, "Truly, I say to you, no sign shall be given to this generation" (8:12). Even false messiahs can work signs and wonders (13:22). A sign does not offer proof but only deceives and diverts attention. Still, we are to watch and be alert, though not for obvious signs. Our vision must be trained to look

130

for the right things, the true signs that point to the true Messiah.

When it trains its vision to see the risen Christ who goes ahead, the church opens itself to seeing the work of God in surprising places.[10] There is no template for discovering what the shape of its findings will be, because every encounter is always new. The only constant component is the presence of a free Christ, boundless and uncontrolled, unrestricted by every attempt to circumscribe his present activity, particularly by those who worship him as Lord. Finding the resurrected one in the unexpected is not a sign that the church has lost confidence in the story it tells, the rites it enacts, or the way of life it has been given. Rather, all of these things are enlisted in sharpening the vision of those within the church for seeing that even the church cannot exhaust the reach of God's kingdom. Christ's reign is not only over the church but over the whole world. The promise to God's people is to rule the world with him, though only because it has been given to them to see how the reign of Christ touches all corners of creation. The pretense of rulers is brought low because Christ has defeated them in his death and resurrection; this means that the church may speak with confidence to those rulers. Oppressed people of all kinds are recipients of the liberation brought by the resurrection; this means not only that the church must go first to the oppressed, but also that it should not be surprised when it finds that Jesus is already there.

Because the church is open to the unexpected movements of Christ in the world, it will welcome the assistance of outsiders. Just as Jesus kept his disciples from forbidding the unnamed exorcist from working in the name of Jesus (9:38–40), so too the church's conviction

10. Jenson, *Systematic Theology* 1:198.

of the resurrection's ultimate reality will not foreclose on the good actions of others. "For truly, I say to you, whoever gives you a cup of water to drink because you bear the name of Christ, will by no means lose his reward" (9:41). Outsiders are brought in because the kingdom extends even to those the church has not yet reached. Therefore, in its witness to the world, the church may be surprised but not ultimately shocked when its message is welcomed rather than rejected. And when this happens, it will not be because the message it proclaims is not somehow "new" but because its truth is deeper than those who proclaim it can grasp. The church remains open to discovering new facets and fresh meanings of the message it carries, not because it doubts the message's truth but precisely because the truth is also a mystery.

The martyr-church is never privileged to maintain a stance of permanent opposition against the world. Because the world has been redeemed and remade in Christ, the church must look for ways that Christ's kingdom has already dawned in the world, transforming hostility into hospitality, converting conflict into concord, and exchanging exclusion for welcome. The martyr-church is prepared to suffer even though it knows that suffering is no longer the shape of the universe. When it suffers, it does not do so because suffering "means something" but precisely because it has lost its meaning as a determinative feature of a world made new by the suffering of Christ. There is no necessary connection between the witness of the church and the suffering of Christians for that witness. There is only the inexplicable reality of a world that continues to resist Christ's reign. The world will not *always* resist the gospel, but its occasional nonresistance is a gift of God's kingdom, an incalculable consequence of the fact that Jesus goes before us into Galilee and beyond.

7

MARTYRDOM
AND PROMISE

ark does not romanticize martyrdom and neither
should we. We are rightly suspicious of a "martyr complex" that preoccupies life with thoughts
of death, particularly dramatic or heroic death. We know
that there is more to the proclamation of the gospel than
the condemnation of the world and that there is thus
more to the Christian life than the provocation of grim
realities, setting the hope of the kingdom of God over
against the fate of the principalities and powers.

However, the reasons we have for refusing to romanticize martyrdom are different from Mark's. Particularly in
the Christian and post-Christian West, it is easy to think
of the church as a servant of the social order by virtue
of its power to act as a director of that order. Christians
are still mostly seen as responsible citizens, pillars of

society, those who are often entrusted with the common good. Martyrdom suggests a set of ideas that run contrary to such an assumption. It suggests that there is a fundamental discontinuity between Christian and other responsibilities. It suggests that loyalties to the kingdom of God are in deep conflict with other loyalties. Not only will we not readily admit that this conflict exists, operating as though it does not, but we may even argue that, as a matter of principle, Christian belief undergirds a form of responsibility that precludes the recklessness that martyrdom names.

But, again, these are not Mark's reasons. Mark does not question the persecution that the church will face but only considers how the church ought to prepare for it. Jesus's warnings to his disciples about his own suffering are not mere dispensations of information or clever predictions about what the future holds for one extraordinary man. If they are true warnings about Jesus himself, they are true warnings for the church as well. At the same time, they are not meant to outline a strategy for avoiding persecution by altering their behavior, guarding their speech, or otherwise disguising their actions.

Instead, they are pedagogical alerts for the purpose of preparation and clarification. Jesus's disciples need to be prepared for the consequences of following Jesus and know the seriousness of their commitments even before they take the first step on the road to Jerusalem. In the course of their following, they need to be trained to meet opposition with determination and fearlessness. In the meantime, it is just as crucial that disciples know whom they are following and the nature of the kingdom over which Jesus is promised to reign. If Jesus were the king of Israel mockingly imagined by the chief priests, he would have done exactly what they said, saving himself by coming down off the cross (15:32). What they could not imagine was that saving one's life requires losing it and that any kingdom might possibly operate that way. Jesus warns his disciples that he will suffer and die, not so that they will resign themselves to the fact that he will never be crowned but so that they will train their sights to see the cross itself as the apex of his glorification. Eyes to see are not just for following Jesus on the road but for recognizing the site of separation, departure, shame, and confusion for what it really is: the site of gathering, overcoming, victory, understanding, and order. Such eyes see the light shining in the darkness even, and especially, at darkness's nadir, having understood the meaning of the light and the false pretense of the darkness.

Mark realistically considers the situation of the church in a hostile world. He does not consider that the church will be called on to rule nations but instead gives considerable attention to the future suffering of the church at the hands of principalities and powers. Before the nations can rejoice and be glad that the God of Jesus Christ reigns, the reign of Jesus Christ in the church provokes the wrath of the nations. In fact, the nations' ability ever to be glad is itself enclosed in the provocation occasioned by Christ's reign. Mark is also realistic about the abusive leaders of the nations, who "lord it over them" (10:42). The way the church exercises authority—as servants—is in contrast to this, with the suffering of the Son of Man functioning as the highest example. But that suffering also confirms that the nations do indeed lord it over their subjects.

Mark's realistic appraisal of the church's opposition is located in the much larger perspective of the meaning of history as eschatologically directed and understood by God who directs that history. Seeing the true meaning of any event involves correctly appraising the connections an event makes with similar events, how it

135

is distinguished from apparently similar events, what causes them, and what follows from them. We know what something is because of how it fits into a category or a sequence. Any available meaning of history would seem to be bounded by these options as well.

But what does it mean to see the meaning of history *eschatologically*? Contrary to what might be assumed, it is not the same as reading a course of events from a privileged standpoint. Instead, it means being released from those categories that supervene on our perception of the world but that serve only to underwrite human pride, idolatry, and resignation to death.[1] Pride says that we determine the course and meaning of history; naming it as pride reveals that we are inaccurate so to assess our status. Idolatry says that we go further than this and entrust our lives to our own historical products; naming this as idolatry reveals that we are sinful and foolish for doing so. Resignation to death says that we have understood the cycle of life and limited our hopes by having taken up our place in it; naming this resignation reminds us that such hopes are too small.

Jesus's warnings are not mere predictions. As predictions, they would seem to tell us something new about the future but in fact would only remind us of the past. We would believe them as predictions because they accord with our predilection for pride, idolatry, and death. We would dismiss them as manifestly false if they violated our understanding of how the world works, of cause and effect, of ranges of possibility, of life and death. Predictions could not stand were they to contravene the more general predictability of the

---

1. There is much to say concerning Nietzsche's famous disdain for Christianity's appeal to history's meaning. However, the greater part of his critique fails to connect with its target once history's meaning is rendered in a properly eschatological idiom.

suffering of the weak, the success of the powerful, the goodness of progress, and the promise of technology to save. Likewise, it is inconceivable that a future event would transgress the temporal requirements for ordinary accomplishments or the collective concord necessary for meaningful work.

Nevertheless, if we could draw conclusions from what happened before, we would not be possessed of the wonder that asks about what happens next. When Jesus speaks about the future life of the church, its suffering witness, he is not inviting his disciples to see with a God's-eye view, abstracted from their time and place. Instead, he is reorienting the present perception of a people for whom the future arrives in temporal succession in the same way as for anybody else. It is not the esoteric knowledge of the events themselves that constitutes Jesus's special insight or the disciples' privilege. It is the *meaning* of the events that characterizes the simultaneous invitation and caution extended to the disciples, the places the events find within the larger story of God's salvation. The stress is precisely *not* on the inevitability of the events but on their surprise, given that the ordinary sequence of events is no longer seen to be decisive. Event followed by event, causally connected by a greater meaning that underwrites the normativity of that meaning—this no longer holds the key to life in the world; it never has.

Therefore, the church's self-knowledge is reoriented through developing the moral skill necessary to perceive that its future suffering is in the hands of God. Jesus does not so much say "This is what the future holds for you" as "If you are able to see, you will see that this future is *your future* when it comes." A great crisis is indicated by the church's inability to recognize itself in what Jesus says about the future for his disciples.

This is not only a modern problem but was in fact true of the disciples in Mark's story: their desertion at the moment of confrontation in Gethsemane, symbolized by the young man who flees naked, signals their inability to understand the nature of the crisis at that moment. And this is no different from the church's absence at the cross in which "Take up your cross and follow me" hauntingly recalls the disciples' having abandoned both crosses and following. The scene is thus marked by death rather than glory, with the exception only of the centurion, who "stood facing him" (15:39) not as a follower (who would not be facing him) but as an executioner who nevertheless spoke a true confession in spite of the church's absence. The women are noted as former followers—they had followed him in Galilee—but now stand at a distance, looking on from afar (15:40–41).

This shows that "You will all fall away" is not an eschatological statement like the promise of future suffering. It is a prediction. Jesus predicts the disciples' weakness, confusion, fear, sleep, and flight, and they rigorously deny it. In contrast, Jesus's statements about suffering are usually met with misunderstanding and bewilderment. When they are met with denial, as in the case of Peter on the road, they are rebuked rather than simply contradicted. Peter's rebuke involved stepping in front of Jesus, physically blocking his forward progress to Jerusalem, which Jesus had just explained means the cross. By doing so, Peter was not contradicting a prediction about what would happen in the Holy City but was positively demonstrating his antagonism to God's history in which crosses find their place only among those who perceive that suffering on them, despite appearances, realizes divine glory. Peter refused to see how this could be the meaning of history. He did not misunderstand Jesus's words about being killed; this was plain enough to him and provoked his indignation. What he did misunderstand were his own words uttered a moment earlier—that Jesus is the Christ. Unlike in Matthew and Luke, Jesus here does not commend Peter for his ostensibly correct confession, since Peter so quickly reveals that he has no idea what a "Christ" is.

Even though both "You will all fall away" and "The Son of man must suffer many things" come to pass, it is important to notice that only the former (a prediction) is unsalutary and a source of the church's shame. The latter (a promise) is the height of the church's glory insofar as it bears the cross with Jesus. This difference is important because it contradicts the ordinary course of such statements. That the disciples fail to stay awake and subsequently flee is not a surprising turn of events for Mark's readers. It merely represents the continuation of events that have gone beforehand. It is causally related to all the other episodes in which the disciples feature. It does not challenge their blindness, but it is the logical outcome of their inability to see. The disciples' failure in crisis does not gainsay their prior fear but confirms and extends it to a higher degree. We are not compelled to ask at Gethsemane what happens next to the disciples, since it is all too obvious from what has gone before. The reader does not question the meaning of these events, for they accord with our accepted views about the way the world works.

But this is not the case when Jesus warns about the disciples' suffering. They will suffer precisely because they do not flee, do not fight against the security forces that come in the night, and do not bear false witness in order to escape punishment. Jesus abstained from all of these things and warned that this too would characterize the life and witness of the church *if the predictions fail.* So long as the church, like the disciples, continues in blindness by following without understanding and then fleeing at the crucial moment, then it will never share in the promise of cruciform suffering in face of the world's unbelief. It will never know the joy of Christ's glory so long as it abandons the weight of the cross, misunderstanding the nature of true glory.

The ability of the church to share in the glory of Christ's suffering resides in its preference for promise over prediction. It discovers that its own unfaithfulness is found in its reliance on standard causality, known by prediction and therefore never known as anything really new or different from what has come before.[2] The church fully deserves its idols. By entrusting itself to its own historical products, it condemns itself to falling away from Jesus—something foretold by him but known by the church only through causal extrapolation. This shows that it is easier to know about forecast than about promise. Forecast is known by trusting the meaning of the past elaborated in the present. It thereby sanctifies human history read idolatrously as our own creation, with the inevitable result of a cosmos that makes no room for crosses. Such a cosmos is the necessary condition for "You will all fall away" to be a true statement.

On the other hand, promise is known by faith, which is enacted in following Jesus into a surprising future. The future is full of surprises because of the freedom of the promise maker to fulfill the promise, and also the persisting presence of the promise maker to those to whom the promise is made. When the church does not share in the glory of Christ's suffering, not only does it think idolatrously about its own existence as an inheritor

2. For an account of how "apocalyptic" reflects the antithesis of standard causality, see David Toole, *Waiting for Godot in Sarajevo: Theological Reflections on Nihilism, Tragedy, and Apocalypse* (Boulder: Westview, 1998).

of history's obvious meaning, but it also refuses the presence of the promise maker, namely, the Spirit of the risen Christ poured out on those who fell away. Such a church doubly denies the resurrection of Christ. It says that there is no surprise so long as its life is characterized by forecast and the determinativeness of its past for its present identity. It also protects itself from encountering the risen Christ by refusing to be surprised. Together, these denials signify a will to know the future without trusting God's promises.[3]

In light of this, there is a further irony. In Mark, the church deserts Jesus at the moment of crisis for the express reason that he appeared impotent or unwilling to deliver on his promises. Surely he had promised more than this. Surely he had displayed greater strength. Had he not promised a kingdom of liberation? Had he not promised to lead his followers to victory?

Jesus's disciples had a selective memory that caused them to remember some promises and not others. They displayed a preference for those aspects of Jesus's authority that they interpreted as victorious in the traditional sense: "With authority he commands even the unclean spirits, and they obey him!" (1:27). But the authority of the servant was consistently misunderstood and conveniently forgotten. Humility was exchanged for superiority—not on the cross but before it; not at the height of glory understood as sacrifice but on the way, abandoning

3. It is crucial that the dialectic of promise and fulfillment does not collapse, since it is precisely insofar as they remain separated that history is possible at all. This is to say that *history* denotes the form that God's promise and fulfillment take, as Hans Urs von Balthasar argues in *A Theology of History* (San Francisco: Ignatius, 1994), 127–33. Put differently again, human history is nothing other than the time between God's promises to his creatures in Christ and their fulfillment, meaning that history is a creation of God, in a sense secondary to (because dependent on) the positive events of promising and presence to the promised.

141

sacrifice. The disciples remembered and misremembered according to their knowledge of how the world works: the strong defeat the weak; when the weak get stronger they will defeat the strong; one kingdom replaces another by force. Despite the actual content of his promises, Jesus could be seen as failing to deliver on his promises of victory only in the minds of disciples for whom the current state of affairs refuses fundamentally to be challenged. His promises were made back into forecasts.

If promises are distinct from forecasts and predictions, they are so because they violate our standard assumptions about instrumentality. If suffering and persecution are promised, this is not for instrumental reasons but on account of the gifts that the promise names: the promise itself and the continuing presence of the promise maker. This suggests another reason that today's church misunderstands martyrdom: it wrongly sees martyrdom as a means to an end, as a proof of something else, as making a kind of statement. This can be seen in what I have said regarding responsibility: where martyrdom comes into conflict with political or social responsibility, the ability to accomplish something better than that which martyrdom accomplishes, martyrdom is misunderstood for the simple fact that it is made to function instrumentally.[4] A martyred church could do so much more good if it refused martyrdom. Martyred parents accomplish one thing by martyrdom but forsake their responsibility to raise their children.[5] The problem with

4. In this regard, the temptation to instrumentalize martyrdom may be seen as a specific instance of the more general temptation Bernd Wannenwetsch suggests besets the church with respect to its worship practices. See his *Political Worship: Ethics for Christian Citizens* (Oxford: Oxford University Press, 2004), esp. 133.

5. The theme of leaving children behind is common in Origen's *Exhortation to Martyrdom*.

objections of this kind is not that they wrongly calculate the good of martyrdom over against some other good but that they mistakenly assume that martyrdom is related instrumentally to goods in the first place.

It is better to speak about martyrdom as itself a gift and not a way of accomplishing something. Martyrs do not die in order to make a point. They do not mean to show the courage of the Christian, the wickedness of the world, the integrity and truth of Christian beliefs, the consistency of moral commitments, or even the fact that God can be trusted. All of these things may be true and may be involved in the mind and actions of the martyr. They may be necessary for the martyr to face death without fear. But they are not the meaning of martyrdom as Jesus promised it would be. In the same way, martyrs do not mean to clarify for the nations the difference between courage and foolishness, nor to show the true meaning of responsibility. Martyrs do not mean to do any of these things: the only thing they *mean* is the meaning their lives and deaths are given by God.[6]

Mark locates the noninstrumentality of martyrdom in the free words offered as testimony by those who are persecuted. "And when they bring you to trial and deliver you up, do not be anxious beforehand what you are to say; but say whatever is given you in that hour, for it is not you who speak, but the Holy Spirit" (13:11). If martyrdom is itself a gift, the words spoken or withheld in the trial are likewise a gift. The lack of anxiety over what to say is also a gift. Anxious speech is speech that

6. See J. P. M. Sweet's analysis of Revelation's disjunction between the possible moral effect of the sufferer and the vindication of God in "Maintaining the Testimony of Jesus: The Suffering of Christians in the Revelation of John," in *Suffering and Martyrdom in the New Testament*, ed. William Horbury and Brian McNeil (Cambridge: Cambridge University Press, 1981), 101–17.

attempts to accomplish something other than itself; it tries to steer the sympathies of the audience in a particular direction; it attempts to articulate only words that will produce the desired effect. Anxious speech cannot countenance saying only what is given, only these words and nothing more. It cannot rest in the peace that comes from not needing to persuade listeners of the truth of the testimony or the innocence of the accused party. Anxious speech is anxious precisely because it tries to manage its results. It controls and manipulates words in attempts to master the truth of its testimony.[7]

The persecuted disciple of Jesus is in a rather odd relationship to noninstrumental testimony. On the one hand, the accused party is clearly the one called on to bear witness. Part of the truth proclaimed is the self-involving character of the proclamation itself. Self-involvement does not prove anything, but because the church only exists by virtue of the content of its proclamation, it cannot speak truthfully without speaking, in this sense, on behalf of itself. If Jesus is risen, then the proclamation "Jesus is risen" is part of the story in which Jesus is risen.[8] Insofar as the church tells this story, therefore, it will have to tell the story *itself*. But on the other hand, even though the accused party bears witness, it is the Spirit who gives the gift of words. This is the sense in which the church decidedly does *not* speak on behalf of itself. It refuses its own intuitions and immediate reactions, does not trust its first response, and curtails its own best

7. See Paul J. Griffiths's exposition of Augustine's treatment of lying according to what he calls "disowning." Griffiths, *Lying: An Augustinian Theology of Duplicity* (Grand Rapids: Brazos, 2004), chap. 5.

8. "The telling of Jesus' Resurrection belongs itself to the narrative by which the resurrection proclamation establishes its own meaningfulness." Robert W. Jenson, *Systematic Theology*, vol. 1, *The Triune God* (Oxford: Oxford University Press, 1997), 175.

efforts to craft its testimony into persuasive speech. In doing this, the church bears witness to God's gifts as continuous realities, ever present to the church, and with special intensity in the moment when it is called on to account for the conditions of its own existence.

Moreover, the truth of a martyr's testimony is like the meaning of the martyr's death: both are gifts. Promise is the way that a gift is known. It is known without being grasped, leaving the promise maker free to fulfill the promise. It is impossible to have a promise without the promise maker.[9] Grasping after promises turns promises into brute knowledge bereft of surprises and alienates the free action of the promise maker. Ultimately grasping actually results in the death of the promise maker, just as the heir in the parable of the vineyard is not just beaten and sent away but killed (12:7–8). A bruised heir will still inherit the vineyard according to the promise of inheritance; the heir's death is the only way to secure tenancy as a possession.

In the same way, a dead Jesus allows for a knowledge of grasping, controlling, and manipulating. Promises are unwound, detached from both their beginning and end. They float free as words and phrases that are made to function according to the logic of convenience, persuasion, defense, and ideology. When they are spoken, it becomes impossible for such words to constitute true testimony because their truth was only ever bound up with the continuing faithfulness of the one who gave them to us. Ironically, the grasping and controlling that

9. This is why, as Guy Mansini argues in *Promising and the Good* (Naples, FL: Sapientia, 2005), a future disclosed through promise depends on trust rather than expertise, which is to say that the relationship of the knower to the promise maker is inevitably bound up with the knowledge of the promise. Therefore, such knowledge can never outlive the relationship (or the promise maker).

released knowledge from promise in hopes of impart-
ing direct access to them has actually worked counter-
productively. Such knowledge may be useful for accomplishing ends, but it can no longer be *true* knowledge, as
direct apprehension is revealed to be a myth in which
what is apprehended is evacuated of anything new or
real. A dead Jesus means dead knowledge.

In contrast, though, the Holy Spirit is the spirit of
the risen Christ, whose presence owes to Jesus's promise to remain with his disciples and not leave them on
their own. The gift that is the Holy Spirit continues to
give the gifts of promise—unexpectedly, provisionally,
and in the moment of need. No gift can be rendered
logically necessary without ceasing to be a gift, which
means that the coming of the Spirit is not apprehended
by knowledge through forecast and prediction but is
contingent on promise. Just as all of creation exists by
sheer gift, just as God did not need to create anything, so
the creation of the church by the Holy Spirit is enacted
by the constant presence of God to the divine promise
to make a holy people. All of the Spirit's gifts, like the
gift of the church, are contingent creations. This is true
of disciples who are called on to bear testimony in front
of governors and kings for the sake of Jesus. There is
no need for disciples to prepare a speech in advance of
their trial, though this is not just a way of relieving them
of a burden. Instead, the nonpreparation for speech at
the trial is itself part of how disciples bear witness to
the resurrection, that Christ has ascended and sent the
Spirit, and that God gives good gifts.

Martyrdom does not cause anything in the way that
we normally suppose that things are caused.[10] That the

10. My debt to Chris K. Huebner's excellent analysis of martyrdom's
noninstrumentality will be evident throughout this chapter. See Huebner, *A*

146

death of martyrs is anything other than utter silence and barrenness does not follow from anything inherent in the fact that some people are willing to die for their beliefs or that some are impressed by the stubborn determination of others. It cannot be known by any accounts of judging cause and effect. There is no measurement for calculating the consequences of such a risky action. Just as martyrs do not act on the basis of this kind of knowledge, martyrdom makes no predictions or forecasts. No knowledge flows from the deaths of martyrs, since martyrdom does not prove anything. Nietzsche was right to point out that it is never necessary to refute a martyr. This is not only because martyrs are silenced but also because even their silence does not make an argument.[11]

Understanding martyrdom noninstrumentally crucially and rightly construes the death of martyrs as continuous with the truth of their testimony. Their boldness in the face of death is not evidence of a more fundamental reality such as the strength of their convictions or the hope of vindication. Instead, a martyr's boldness is itself part of noninstrumental testimony. Death does not put an end to testimony; death is part of the testimony. Speaking about martyrdom instrumentally relies on instrumentalizing testimony more generally, but this is precisely what is not allowed. Martyrdom is not a special case or specific category of bearing witness to the gospel. It is simply the form that witness often takes when it does not seek to accomplish anything through testimony. In a setting where martyrdom is rare, the question at least must be asked: have we instrumental-

---

Precarious Peace: Yoderian Explorations on Theology, Knowledge, and Identity (Scottsdale, PA: Herald, 2006), esp. chap. 8.

11. Friedrich Nietzsche, *The Antichrist*, in *The Portable Nietzsche*, ed. and trans. by Walter Kaufman (London: Viking Penguin, 1968), sec. 53.

ized testimony? Detached for grasping, such testimony quite simply cannot be true.[12]

We call "tragic" those who suffer for things that are not true. This reveals two things that have been suggested above. First, it suggests that suffering for something does not guarantee the truth of that thing. The pathology of a martyr complex is often a heavy-handed attempt to escape the vulnerability of speaking the truth without the means of convincing others that it is true. It signifies impatience with the freedom of others not to believe. It betrays an insecurity that cannot bear its own knowledge without compulsion for everyone else. In a word, it expresses doubt. Such doubt may explain why martyrdom is sometimes misconstrued and applied to deaths of fighters. For the New Testament, martyrs do not die because they fight for what is right but precisely because they *refuse* to fight for what is true. A fighter fundamentally doubts whether his truth is true and anxiously grasps at it, preferring secure knowledge to uncertain promise made certain only through faith. Fighters do not stand by the truth of their convictions.

Second, the tragedy of those who suffer for untrue things is actually deeper than this. The real tragedy is that suffering-as-proof does in fact prove something, though it cannot help but prove something that is sadly much more mundane and tedious than it hopes to. If martyrs could prove the truth—that is, if their suffering is thought of as suffering *for*—then the object of their suffering is revealed only to be something that can be known apart from contingent promise and gift. The object is thought of as logically necessary where martyrdom functions as

12. But we may not reverse the logic in efforts somehow to prove the truth of testimony on the basis that we have not instrumentalized it, since to do this would, in fact, be to instrumentalize it.

148

an instrumental step in a logical argument that results in a conclusion.[13] But since such truths are subject to a kind of knowing that is conditioned by cause and effect, the convictions for which the martyr dies are exposed as recycled insights monotonously paraded as new and liberating.

Knowing this, however, cannot be reversed. Disqualifying one claim as tragic because it instrumentalizes does not validate its opposite. It does not show that noninstrumentalized claims are true. In fact, noninstrumentalized claims are decidedly marked by their status as contingent, open to refutation, vulnerable, and not necessarily true. Martyrdom does not prove the truth, but it is difficult to see how something could be true if it did not produce martyrs—those who not only do not die *for* their convictions but who, more importantly, refuse to fight for them. This does not mean that true martyrs are true only if they believe that their beliefs might be false. Rather, the martyr's conviction of the truth is described by a kind of knowledge that believes God's promises and welcomes God's gifts. It is irrespective of any intrinsic quality of those beliefs and convictions that says that they must be believed by every rational person.

Mark's reasons for refusing to romanticize martyrdom are different from ours. This is especially the case when we make martyrdom into an argument, in which case it is no surprise when we imitate commensurate ways

13. This is no doubt why Barth comments that "one cannot try to be a martyr. One can only be ready to be made a martyr." *Church Dogmatics* 3/4, trans. G. W. Bromiley et al. (Edinburgh: T & T Clark, 1956–75), 79. As I have observed before, to be a martyr is a special occurrence of opposition that calls on individuals who respond; it is not a permanent feature of the opposition between belief and unbelief, no matter how permanent that opposition itself may be. Even so, such an opposition is never necessary, it just happens to be so. Occasional martyrdom witnesses to the conviction that Christian witness has no *necessary* quarrel with anything.

of knowing absent the attendant risk of death. Not only do we refuse to romanticize martyrdom, but we also positively reject it in favor of seemingly stronger forms of necessity and force, more compelling apologetics, more universally appealing knowledge. But Revelation's scroll remains tightly sealed to this kind of grasping. It cannot be opened except by one whose ability to open the scroll is itself a surprise of contingent gift, the gift of glory and power from the Father to the Son, the slain Lamb. Only the Lamb is declared worthy to break the seals and read out the contents: the martyr-witness of the church is used by God to bring about the repentance of the nations.[14] This is an instrumentality of sheer promise, of gift. The death of martyrs has meaning in history because of the worth of the Lamb to open the scroll. The glory of their witness is continuous with the presence of God to creation all the way through to the redemption of the fallen nations, precisely by way of those whose deaths expose the violence of the powers. Knowing that those who suffer because of true testimony pivot at the site of death and life is possible only for a church that persists in knowing the meaning of history through the cross and resurrection of Christ, for those who sing the new song of promise while the Lamb opens seals—a song only they can sing. It is for those who know it is given to silenced martyrs to sing the loudest chorus.

14. See Richard Bauckham, *The Theology of the Book of Revelation* (Cambridge: Cambridge University Press, 1993), 84.

Scripture Index

Subject Index

153